A JAPANESE TOUCH FOR THE SEASONS

A JAPANESE TOUCH FOR THE SEASONS

Kunio Ekiguchi
Ruth S. McCreery

KODANSHA INTERNATIONAL
Tokyo and New York

The craft projects presented in these pages were created specially for this book by Kunio Ekiguchi, who also originated the book concept. Ruth S. McCreery wrote the essays.

Photographs of craft projects by Akihiko Tokue. Line drawings by Eiko Ikeda.

Distributed in the United States by Kodansha International/USA Ltd., 114 Fifth Avenue, New York, New York 10011.

Published by Kodansha International Ltd., 2-2, Otowa 1-chome, Bunkyo-ku, Tokyo 112 and Kodansha International/USA Ltd., 114 Fifth Avenue, New York, New York 10011.

Library of Congress Cataloging-in-Publication Data
Ekiguchi, Kunio, 1930–
    A Japanese touch for the seasons.
    Includes index.
    1. Handicraft—Japan. 2. Seasons. I. McCreery,
Ruth S. (Ruth South), 1946– . II. Title.
TT105.E39 1987 745.594'1'0952 86-40431
ISBN 0-87011-811-0

CONTENTS

AUTUMN 秋

WINTER 冬

Introduction: Living with the Seasons

In the Japanese world view, all natural and social events are fully savored and take on their proper meaning only in the context of the season. This sense of season is a perception of temporal flow and the rhythms of nature that forms the ground from which life derives meaning.

The Japanese attitude toward the seasons is most clearly seen in the haiku, Japan's distinctive poetic form of seventeen syllables. Haiku conventions require each concise verse to contain a seasonal theme that evokes the background for the two specific images presented and that expands their meaning beyond the particular. At the same time, the moment caught by those images should reveal something fresh and unexpected about the season itself. The interplay between the seasonal theme and the specific images makes the season simultaneously the wider context of the poem's meaning and its subject.

The use of the seasons as the essential context for specific events is so deeply rooted an aspect of Japanese culture that Japanese often comment on how unique their country is in having four distinct seasons, a statement that leaves visitors from other temperate regions speechless or puzzled. The Japanese attitude is not arrogance or ignorance. While there is nothing remarkable about having four seasons, they are certainly experienced differently in Japan.

Seasonal signs are eagerly noted. This includes not only the arrival of the first bush warbler in spring or the turning of the maple leaves in fall, but humbler signs of cyclical change—wild grasses sprouting, mackerel glistening in the fish market, the sound of wooden clogs modulating from a brisk clack on winter's frozen earth to a gentler clopping in spring. The changing length of the day is, of course, a significant seasonal marker, but so are shadows, which change in length and blackness according to the time of the year. An attenuated February shadow defines the season and mood quite specifically in Japan.

With this detailed observation of the seasons comes their introduction into daily life. The foods served and their preparation are adjusted to the season, so much so that cookbooks are often organized by season. A dish strongly associated with one season, as one-pot stews are with winter, is almost inedible out of its proper season. Similarly, Japanese cooks have a strong preference for fresh vegetables in season. Frozen and canned vegetables, with their bland lack of seasonality, have little place in most Japanese kitchens.

Clothing, too, is changed with the seasons, not only to keep the wearer comfortable but to create a sense of seasonal awareness. Those who follow this custom too strictly may be seen sweating in fur coats on a balmy day designated as the first day of winter according to the calendar.

Not only people but also houses don different coverings with the turn of seasons. The greatest contrasts in interior furnishings are between summer and winter—between displays of airy coolness and cozy warmth—but smaller seasonal adjustments are made constantly in the choice of paintings displayed, dishes used, flowers arranged, and ornaments on view.

Celebrations and festivals, whether New Year's or Boys' Day, are also closely associated with their respective seasons, a linkage heightened by incorporating seasonal foods and decorations from nature into the festivities. Many of Japan's festivals originated in rites observed at critical points in the agricultural cycle, which is no doubt a source of their focus on nature.

As an agricultural society, the Japanese had to anticipate the changing seasons. Early rules of thumb must have been derived from plant and animal signs. A natural guide to planting times, for instance, can be based on observing flowering plants: when forsythia and Siberian squill are in bloom, it is safe to plant onions and peas, but eggplant and watermelon must wait for the azaleas and peonies to bloom. The complex agriculture of wet rice farming, however, required more planning ahead. It called for a workable calendar that applied everywhere and that everyone could understand.

Traditionally Japan used two calendars: an official lunar calendar and an unofficial solar one, both borrowed from China. Lunar calendars define the month to correspond closely to the phases of the moon. In the version used in Japan, the first day of the month was the new moon, and the full moon fell on the fifteenth. This lunar calendar was simple to read from the night sky. Unfortunately, the moon affects only tides and lovers, not the seasons. To represent accurately the annual cycle of growth and decay, a calendar must fit the earth's rotation around the sun. Since twelve lunar months fall twelve or so days short of the solar year, a lunar calendar tends to slip rapidly out of synchronization with the natural seasons unless adjusted in some way.

Instead of the simple, but unreliable, lunar calendar, Japan's farmers relied on a solar calendar. Defining a year as the interval between two winter solstices, the old solar calendar divides the year into twenty-four approximately equidistant points, or *sekki*, that serve as seasonal markers. Each point has a name, usually referring to the weather or to agricultural phenomenon. Unfortunately, since the names were borrowed from China with the calendar, they only rarely apply to conditions in Japan. The End of Insect Hibernation, March 5 or 6, for instance, is still much too cold for most insects in Japan to venture forth. The Greater Heat, which falls on July 23 or 24, actually comes well before the hottest summer weather. Perhaps somewhere in China the weather patterns fit these names, but in Japan they are endlessly confusing.

Inappropriate as their names may be, the twenty-four seasonal markers do constitute a simple, accurate solar calendar, a good guide to weather for planting and harvesting. Moreover, this solar calendar served as an anchor that tied the lunar calendar to some contact with the reality of the seasons. The lunar eleventh month was, by definition, the month in which the winter solstice occurred. The twelfth month, similarly, had to include the seasonal marker called the Greater Cold, which falls on January 20 or 21. Lunar New Year's Day was the first new moon after the Greater Cold; that limited its range of variation to between January 21 and February 19.

Years were also counted in various ways, including the Chinese system of ten stems and twelve branches. The ten stems are the five elements of wood, fire, earth, metal, and water, in their yin and yang aspects, and the twelve branches are the twelve animals: rat, ox, tiger, rabbit, dragon, snake, horse, sheep, monkey, rooster, dog, and boar. Together the two ordered sets yield the sixty combinations that make up the sexagenary cycle. The year 1987, for example, is the fourth year in the cycle, the year of the yin aspect of fire and the year of the rabbit. The same cycle of sixty combinations was used to designate the days.

Japan adopted the Western, or Gregorian, solar calendar on January 1, 1873, and has officially used only that calendar since. While the lunar calendar is still calculated and given in almanacs, most annual festivals and observances that once were regulated by it are now performed according to the Gregorian calendar. Girls' Day, once the third day of the third lunar month, is now celebrated on the third of March. Shifting New Year's from its lunar occurrence near the Establishment of Spring (February 4 or 5) to its present-day solar orientation created more disparity. New Year's greetings still read "New Spring," a remnant of the lunar celebration, but the weather is just moving into the heart of winter.

The calendar shift combined with Japan's rapid conversion from an agricultural to a post-industrial society has necessarily changed the nature of festivals and holidays, yet it is hard to imagine that life in Japan will ever entirely lose its seasonal context. Modern-day pocket calendars still list the *sekki* as well as appropriate seasonal greetings with which to begin writing a letter.

The constant reference to the seasons makes each event—in the manner of haiku—both absolutely particular and resonant with a wider world of meaning. Dwelling upon the seasonal signs of change deepens the joys of each day, makes its transience more painful, yet raises it to a new level of beauty—the poignant beauty of transience itself. High on tristesse, sensitive to the nuances in shadows, those who bring the natural seasons into their lives dare to open themselves up to a richer well of memory and experience.

This book describes the Japanese seasons not as meteorological phenomena but as part of a Japanese way of life. What this book presents in the foods, fauna and flora, festivals, activities, and crafts of each season is less a field guide to what the Japanese do, and when, than an essay on a Japanese approach to living, a way of bringing nature's temporal flow and grand cyclical rhythms into human life. It is also an invitation to try some Japanese seasonal practices—hunting wild edible plants in spring, saluting a person on his having completed a full sixty-year cycle, treating the household to a presentation of coolness in summer, creating dolls to celebrate the birth of a girl. And perhaps then to go beyond the boundaries of Japanese perceptions to find a personal calendar of the seasons and bring them, with their beauty, their ties to all of nature, and the poignancy of their passing, into your own life.

A Note on the Craft Projects

The craft projects in this book range from simple paperfolding to intermediate carpentry, from a fun few minutes of creativity a young child can enjoy to more time-consuming construction of home interior decorations. Before beginning a project, read completely through the instructions to get an idea of the materials and time required. Be sure to supervise children in the construction and operation of such items as the shadow lantern.

BASIC TOOLS AND SUPPLIES: Most of the tools and supplies required are common household items, so they are not listed separately with each set of instructions. Tools typically called for are scissors, a ruler, an X-acto (or paper-cutting) knife, a pencil, brushes, an awl, and a needle. Supplies include glue (see below), tape, tracing paper, thread, and string. Any special tools or supplies required are listed in the instructions for each project.

GLUE: Liquid white glue is suitable for most paper-to-paper bonds. When gluing a large sheet of paper, dilute the white glue with water to the consistency of cream and apply it with a brush. Lightly spray the paper with water to dampen it before brushing on the glue. Wheat starch glue (*shofu nori*), which is preferred in Japan for gluing together large sheets of paper, provides a strong, flexible, nonstaining bond. For joining wood to wood, use wood glue.

PAPER: The papers used in this book can be divided into four types:

1. Thin paper. Any thin, translucent paper, including cellophane, crepe paper, tissue paper, and some Japanese papers such as *usumino*.
2. Medium-weight paper. Typing paper, stationery, origami paper, most wrapping paper, pages from magazines or newspapers, and some Japanese papers such as *hanshi* (a category of papers made from paper mulberry) and *chiyogami* (decorative patterned paper).
3. Heavy paper. Thick, but still flexible, paper, including some wrapping paper and *momigami* (a heavy, crinkled Japanese paper).
4. Cardboard. Heavy card stock, such as that used for shoe boxes and other commercial packing, posterboard, and mat board.

Medium-weight paper is the main material of most projects. Where "paper" is given in the list of materials with no particular weight specified, use medium-weight paper.

Washi, or traditional Japanese paper (preferably handmade), is available in a variety of weights and types. Its strength, range of colors and patterns, flexibility, and characteristic texture make it overwhelmingly preferred for use in paper crafts in Japan. All projects in this book were made with *washi*, but this by no means requires you to do the same; you can easily reproduce the look with Western papers if you wish. Several types of *washi* recommended for use in these projects are *hanshi*, *momigami*, *chiyogami*, *usumino*, and *shojigami* (shoji paper). See the appendix for U.S. suppliers of *washi*.

MIZUHIKI: These dyed cords of twisted paper, called for in several projects, usually come in pairs of colors: red-and-white and gold-and-silver are the most auspicious combinations. A five-strand thickness is standard, although strands can be bought singly or in thicknesses of more strands (always in odd numbers). Their length varies. Nowadays, you can find cheaper varieties of *mizuhiki* consisting of thin paper foil wrapped around a twisted paper core. In some projects, you can successfully substitute fine, stiff ribbon or stiff gift-wrapping cord for *mizuhiki*. See appendix for U.S. suppliers of genuine *mizuhiki*.

To make your own *mizuhiki*, all you need is heavy-weight crochet cotton, poster paint, and gesso. Cut the crochet cotton into the desired number of strands, each an inch longer than the final length needed. Thin the gesso with water to the consistency of cream. Dissolve poster colors in some gesso and then either dip the strands in the gesso or paint the gesso on the strands with a brush. Stretch the strands straight on a flat surface and pin or tape the ends to keep the strands taut. Let them dry for an hour or more before use.

SYMBOLS USED IN THE INSTRUCTIONS:

— — — — — — — — — — — — — — — —

Valley fold. A line of dashes indicates the inside of a fold line. Fold the paper toward you.

— · — · — · — · — · — · — · — · —

Mountain fold. A line of dots and dashes indicates the outside of a fold line. Fold the paper away from you.

✂ ————————————————

A scissors sign (often accompanied by a solid line) indicates a cutting line or point.

SPRING

early February
through
early May

In the personal calendar of many residents of Japan, spring begins with the blooming of the sweet daphne, or *jinchoge*, in early March. Sweet daphne is not one of the grand flowers of Japanese tradition: few poems have been written to its sweet scent and its tiny white blossoms are rarely, if ever, used as a decorative motif. Perhaps these compact bushes are too straightforward in their charms to stir the poet's imagination, but most families do have one in their gardens, and those without gardens often grow one in a pot. In early spring, their powerful sweet perfume intoxicates whole neighborhoods, luring people outside to enjoy the rich scent with its promise that spring is, at last, truly on its way.

The orthodox calendar, however, puts the beginning of spring—the seasonal marker called the Establishment of Spring—much earlier, on February 4 or 5. Hardly springlike, February is actually the coldest month, with gray skies that make the chill feel far more penetrating than in sunny December and January. Early February is also plum-blossom time. It would be easy to admire the lovely plum blossoms, scattered against the black bark of an ancient tree, clinging to it with fragile strength—if it were not so cold outside.

The *uguisu*, or bush warbler, is, however, unhesitating in its attraction to plum blossoms. The warbler's normal diet is insects, but in spring it will leave its preferred bamboo thickets to sip the plum blossoms' nectar. The first *uguisu*, like the first robin in other countries, is thus a harbinger of spring, but more know this small and active bird by sound than by sight. Its distinctive song, a low whistle followed by three loud syllables—*hohokekyo*—begins to ring out in February and March, as the nesting season approaches.

From mid-February on, the plum blossoms and *uguisu* are joined by the bolder beauty of the camellia, and then both delicate plum and fleshy camellia blossoms are battered by *haru ichiban*, the first wind of spring, which sweeps in around February 22. A violent wind that sends hats and laundry flying, *haru ichiban* blows from south to north, ending the winter weather pattern of Siberian air masses settling successively upon Japan from the north. From then on the weather will be changeable but gradually warming.

March brings the fragrant sweet daphne, the Doll Festival, income tax returns, and a rush of advertisements marking the end and beginning of the fiscal and school years. The school year ends around the vernal equinox (March 21 or 22), one of the two days each year when day and night are of the same length. In both spring and fall, the week with the equinox as its midpoint is known as Higan, which now is celebrated as a time of Buddhist memorial services. During Higan, families may have a priest come to chant sutras at their home altar. Special services are held at temples as well, and families gather to visit their family graves, cleaning them, making offerings of flowers, incense, and food, and praying.

Higan, like all Japanese holidays, has its special foods. *O-hagi*, ovals of glutinous rice coated with sweet bean paste, are closely identified with Higan. Another Higan food is *kusa dango*, small balls of glutinous rice flavored with the fragrant herb mugwort (*yomogi*), which is ready to pick around the spring equinox.

Higan is written with Japanese characters meaning "the farther shore," signifying a desire to achieve enlightenment. The emphasis has shifted, however, from trying to attain enlightenment oneself during Higan to helping the deceased pass from the world of confusion (this shore) to the world of enlightenment (the farther shore).

While most Buddhist holidays celebrated in Japan have their roots in China, Higan does not. It appears to be a Japanese innovation that was perhaps a ritual at the start of the critical planting and harvesting seasons. Perhaps this origin is what makes Higan more of a pleasant, relaxing holiday than a solemn time to commemorate the dead.

The weather also contributes to the holiday atmosphere: "Winter cold and summer heat end at Higan," says one adage. Soon after the vernal equinox, it has warmed enough to coax the cherry blossoms into bloom, usually at the beginning of April. Flower viewing is followed by *hana matsuri*, or the Flower Festival.

Hana matsuri is the celebration of the birth of the historical Buddha, Sakyamuni. In most of Japan it is observed on April 8, although some districts celebrate on May 8, to approximate the original lunar date. Temples set up a Flower Hall, a small pavilion roofed in gay flowers. Inside is a miniature statue of the Buddha as an infant. Worshipers use a bamboo ladle to pour sweet tea over the statue, in remembrance of the first bath given the newborn Sakyamuni by nine dragons spouting pure water.

By the middle of April, the world, still brown and barren at Higan, is covered with brilliant green. The azaleas, rhododendrons, deutzias, magnolias—all announce that spring is truly here. On sunny days, winter clothing is aired, then packed away. New babies and toddlers suddenly appear, led by grandparents taking them out to enjoy the sun.

The peak of spring comes on *hachiju-hachiya*, the eighty-eighth day after the Establishment of Spring. Falling on May 2 or 3, *hachiju-hachiya* is a critical date for farmers, for it is usually the last day of frost. From then, farmers are busy with their planting. *Hachiju-hachiya* is also the peak time for tea picking, a major event in this tea-drinking nation. Tea does not have to travel vast distances, roasted and dried, packed in little tins. Here tea is a local product, sold in bulk from large wooden boxes at tea specialty shops found in every community. In fact, rural families may have their own plants, which they pick and take to the village cooperative for drying and subsequent home consumption. *Hachiju-hachiya* means that soon stores will be filled with green mounds of this year's tea, with its fresh and tempting fragrance of spring.

By May 4 or 5, the last day of spring in Japan, the weather is finally balmy. Instead of beginning with something Westerners would call spring weather, spring in the Japanese calendar moves from the coldest days of the year to the intoxicatingly fragrant, warm days of early May. By noticing and appreciating every flower's turn to bloom, every returning bird, every seasonal festival, the Japanese savor the unfolding season as the experience of spring itself.

The Seasons of Spring

RISSHUN 立春

The first spring seasonal marker is *risshun*, or the Establishment of Spring, on February 4 or 5. Despite its name, *risshun* actually is the coldest and gloomiest part of winter, though plum blossoms usually begin blooming soon thereafter. The lunar New Year usually falls near this day.

USUI 雨水

Usui, or Rainwater, follows on February 19 or 20. Its name implies that snow and ice should be giving way to rain. Temperatures may rise somewhat, but the accompanying moister air brings more snow, not rain, to Japan's Snow Country in the north.

KEICHITSU 啓蟄

March 5 or 6 is *keichitsu*, the End of Insect Hibernation, though Japanese insects sensibly ignore it. The first herbs of spring begin to sprout.

SHUNBUN 春分

Shunbun, the vernal equinox, falls on March 21 or 22 and usually marks the end of wintry weather. The first butterflies emerge.

SEIMEI 清明

By *seimei*, or Pure and Clear, on April 5 or 6, the cherry trees are usually blooming. The Chinese custom of cleaning graves on this date is not observed; Japanese do that in the week surrounding *shunbun*.

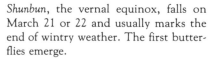

KOKUU 穀雨

April 20 or 21 brings *kokuu*, or Grain Rains, another misnomer. The fifteen-day season beginning with *kokuu* includes *hachiju-hachiya*, the end of frosts and beginning of planting. Spring, warm and fragrant with flowers and new foliage, is at last really here—just as the six spring seasons are over.

Spring means fresh stimulation to every sense. The powerful perfume of the sweet daphne scents the breeze, the low whistle of the bush warbler echoes from the plum trees, and colorful blossoms dazzle the eye. The outdoors is vibrant and irresistible.

bush warbler (*uguisu*)

plum blossoms (*ume*)

peach blossoms (*momo*)

rape blossoms (*nanohana*)

sweet daphne (*jinchoge*)

The warmth of spring brings new growth to field, forest, and bamboo grove. Hunting down edible buds, shoots, and grasses makes for a pleasant spring outing. Be sure to gather these rapidly growing plants in early spring while they are young and tender.

horsetail (*tsukushi*)

wild onion (*nobiru*)

flowering fern (*zenmai*)

water dropwort (*seri*)

bamboo shoots (*takenoko*)

Bamboo shoots (*left*) and wild mountain vegetables (*below*) are at their tastiest in spring.

Flavors of Spring

The reawakening of the earth after winter's hibernation is the theme of Japan's spring foods—the new sprouts, buds, shoots, and blossoms symbolizing the season are sought for their fresh taste of spring.

The search for spring foods begins seriously in March and April, when those who like to savor the season can be seen studying the ground in gardens and alongside roads. It is time for *tsumikusa*, or fresh-picked spring herbs. Some may be available in stores, but the point of *tsumikusa* is the direct encounter of the food gatherer with the warming earth. The wild herbs thus stalked include the stems of *nobiru* (wild onion), the flower buds of *fuki* (butterbur), and the leaves of *yomogi* (artemisia or mugwort), *hakobe* (chickweed), *tanpopo* (dandelion), *kuko* (Chinese matrimony vine), and *seri* (dropwort). The list of edible herbs is limited only by the gatherer's botanical knowledge. Many are thought to be medicinal— mugwort for the stomach and for colds, Chinese matrimony vine as a tonic, chickweed as a tonic especially good for nursing mothers. The aromatic young leaves of mugwort are what season the green rice cakes (*kusa mochi*) of the Doll Festival and the green rice balls (*kusa dango*) of Higan. Many of these hardy plants can even be found in urban neighborhoods, where they are harvested by sharp-eyed cooks with a taste for the earthy flavor of spring.

To bring out their fresh flavors, spring herbs are usually prepared simply. The tender buds, shoots, or flowers are floated in soup or added to salad; blanched, seasoned with bean paste and sesame seeds, and served on rice; or lightly parboiled and served with a drop of soy sauce. Tender young herbs have a slight tang stimulating to the appetite, but older leaves or buds become tough and unpleasantly bitter. The pleasures of spring herbs are only for those who can catch them young.

The more adventurous may head to the woods and mountains to hunt for "mountain vegetables" (*sansai*), wild edible plants such as *warabi* (fiddlehead ferns), *zenmai* (sprouts of a flowering fern), and *yama udo* (shoots of a celery-like plant). Mountain vegetables are often lightly pickled and enjoyed throughout the year as a topping for noodles or as a side dish.

The ultimate spring vegetable is the bamboo shoot (*takenoko*), available fresh only for a few weeks each spring when the warmth of the soil and the length of the day send the shoots thrusting rapidly upward.

The true flavor of the bamboo shoot is, they say, only to be enjoyed out in the bamboo grove. The connoisseur builds a fire of dried leaves over a shoot on the verge of bursting through the ground, steams it where it grows, then digs it up and devours it on the spot. Failing that, the trick is to cook the freshest possible shoots, for they start toughening as soon as they are harvested. Just trim the bottom, cut one long gash through the leaf sheath, and simmer until tender (one to two hours). Then the bamboo shoot can be peeled, chopped, and cooked with rice; left whole (if it is a small, shapely shoot) and simmered in saké, soy sauce, and sugar; sliced into salad; stir-fried with mushrooms—whatever sounds good. The crisp texture and distinctively fresh flavor of the bamboo shoot give every dish a taste of spring.

The Doll Festival

Near the end of February, the best room in a Japanese household with daughters is transformed. The room may ordinarily be a demonstration of restrained good taste, a tranquil combination of natural wood, tatami matting, neutral walls, and minimal furnishings. For a brief season, however, it explodes into an expression of the other side of the Japanese aesthetic—a lavish display of pure color, gold, elaborate designs, and intricate detail. The room has been taken over by the *hina matsuri*, or Doll Festival, display.

The Doll Festival is celebrated on March 3 (formerly on the third day of the third lunar month), even though the dolls can be put on display up to two weeks earlier. According to superstition, if you hope to marry your daughters off, you should not leave the doll display up after the third. It is hard, however, for little girls to let the dolls be packed away, and families often end up letting them overstay the deadline.

The Doll Festival centers on a display of elaborate dolls called *hina ningyo*. The essential figures are the *dairi-sama*, or emperor and empress dolls, usually seated figures wearing the dress of the Heian court (794–1185)—many-layered costumes ending in outer garments of rich brocade. The emperor and empress dolls are backed by a decorative screen, usually gold. Offerings of *hishi mochi*, a pink, white, and green, diamond-shaped cake of glutinous rice paste, are displayed with the dolls, as are *hina arare*, sweetened pink and white puffed rice, and *shiro-zake*, saké mixed with rice malt, a mildly alcoholic sweet drink.

A more fully developed display includes perhaps fifteen dolls, including the ladies-in-waiting, musicians, guards, and attendants for emperor and empress. The possibilities for their accoutrements are almost unlimited. Miniature mandarin orange and cherry trees, like those that grew outside the ancient imperial palace, are usual. So are little lanterns that really light up, set on both sides of the emperor and empress dolls. There are also ceremonial trays, saké sets, tea sets, chests for clothing, and possibly a miniature sewing box. The dolls are also provided with transport, usually an oxcart like that used by the Heian aristocracy and sometimes a palanquin. Everything is made of lacquer (or shiny plastic resembling lacquer). The most beautiful antique sets are decorated lavishly with gold leaf. All the dolls and their furnishings are arranged on tiers of shelves covered with bright red cloth, the emperor and empress dolls at the top. The total effect is simply dazzling.

The bright pink of peach blossoms makes a shocking contrast with the red cloth, but an arrangement of peach blossoms is obligatory. In fact, Peach Blossom Festival is another name for the Doll Festival. The association of peach blossoms with the festival is probably Chinese in origin, for the peach in China was thought to give protection against evil and even grant eternal life. The same beliefs were current in ninth- to twelfth-century Japan, where a branch of peach blossoms or a peach-wood bow could avert evil and the peach—flower, leaf, and kernel—was regarded as medicinal. Then it was customary on the third day of the third month to bathe in water in which peach blossoms had been steeped and to drink peach wine.

On March 3 in modern times, girls invite their friends over to help celebrate the festival. They sit before the display, dressed up in kimono (if their mothers have the patience), to admire the dolls. The lanterns are lit, and the girls sing a lovely song describing the dolls and their accoutrements and eat the *hishi mochi* and puffed rice with the *shiro-zake*. That may be followed by a party meal,

Standing dolls (instructions on p. 127) are the oldest form of paper *hina* dolls. Represented here are a high-ranking samurai and his wife. Arranged in a box shaped like *hishi mochi* sweets, these *noshi* dolls (p. 21) are usually given by grandparents to a granddaughter for the girl's first Doll Festival. The dolls are tucked into a *noshi*, the folded paper traditionally attached to gifts.

A pair of dolls, one male and one female, forms the center-piece for the Doll Festival display. White paper Genji dolls (instructions on p. 20) embody the elegance of the Heian-period imperial court. This pair might be the Shining Prince of the *Tale of Genji* and his wife.

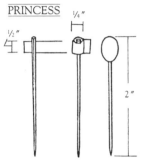

GENJI DOLLS

color photograph on p. 18

MATERIALS

FOR EACH DOLL

head:
bamboo skewer, 2 ¾″ long   paper strip, ⅜″ × 12″
clay, ½″ dia. ball   gesso

base: white *momigami* (or heavy paper), 8 ¼″ × 10″

FOR PRINCESS

collar:
white paper, ¾″ × 2 ½″
pink paper, ¾″ × 2 ½″

headdress:
gold paper, 2″ × 3″
thin wire
beads

kimono:
white *momigami*, 7 ½″ × 23″
pink paper, 7 ½″ × 23″
white paper, 7 ½″ × 23″

FOR PRINCE

collar: 2 strips white paper, each ¾″ × 2 ½″

kimono:
white *momigami*, 7 ½″ × 23″
2 sheets white paper, each 7 ½″ × 23″

headdress:
2 strips gold paper, ½″ × 1 ½″ and ¼″ × 2 ½″
2 strips white paper, ⅛″ × ¼″ and ¼″ × 2 ¾″
toothpick

PRINCESS

1. To make head, wrap paper strip around one end of bamboo skewer until roll is about ¼″ in diameter; glue in place. Cover with clay and smooth into head shape. When clay is dry, coat it with gesso. Allow to dry, and draw in hair and face with sumi ink or paint.

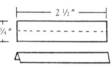

2. Fold collar papers as shown, overlap on the skewers, and glue in place one at a time. Pink strip goes on top.

3. Stack the three sheets for kimono, with *momigami* on bottom and white on top. Cut out a triangular opening as shown, and fold in half. (For prince's kimono, cut out rectangular opening.)

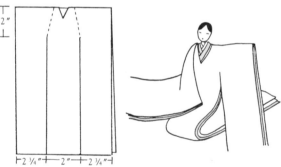

4. Cut through all layers of kimono to form sleeves. Slip kimono over doll's head; fold sleeves forward.

5. Fold base paper lengthwise in thirds and glue closed. Bend kimono into kneeling posture and place base behind "knees." Arrange sleeves in waves and glue in place one at a time where they contact base and each other. Apply glue to underside of base and glue to single layer of kimono (to prevent doll from falling over).

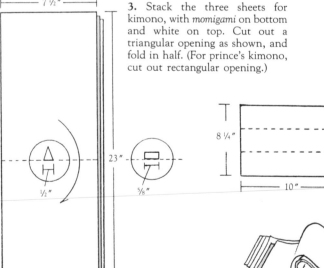

glue

glue

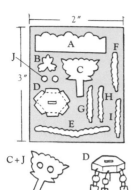

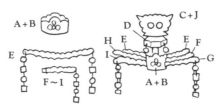

1. Follow steps 1-5 above, substituting materials for prince.

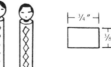

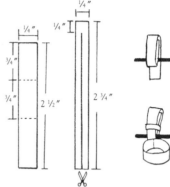

2. To make prince's headdress, fold shorter gold paper strip in half and glue into ring shape.

6. Cut out headdress pieces. Glue two J pieces to piece C. Fold down flaps on D; string each of six wires with a bead and a ⅛" square of gold paper and attach one wire to each flap. Insert tab of C into hole in D.

7. Form ring with A, gluing closed, and glue B to its front. String beads and gold paper squares on wires and attach to both ends of E and rounded ends of F, G, H, and I. Glue midpoint of E to back of A. Arrange pieces F-I at even intervals around A and glue tabs to A. Glue protruding tab of the top assembled in step 6 to inside front of ring formed with A. Tie string around head with bow under chin; fix in place with drop of glue on top of head and under chin. Place headdress on princess and glue in place.

3. Fold other gold paper as shown, gluing 1" piece of toothpick in place. Glue ⅛" wide strip of white paper around folded paper. Glue extending tab to back of ring made in step 9. Make streamers from other strip of white paper and glue to back of ring. Tie and glue string around head as with princess. Place headdress on prince and glue in place.

NOSHI DOLLS

color photograph on p. 19

MATERIALS

heads: same as for Genji Dolls (p. 20)

kimonos: 2 sheets white paper, each 2 ¾" × 4"

hat: gold paper, ⅜" × ¾"

holder:
white, pink, and purple paper, each 5 ⅝" square
5-strand gold-and-silver *mizuhiki*, 22" long

box:
2 sheets cardboard, each 5 1/16" × 7 ¾"
blue *momigami* (or heavy paper), 5 ½" × 8"
red *momigami* (or heavy paper), 5 ½" × 8"
2 sheets wood-grain printed paper, each 6" × 11"

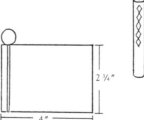

1. Follow step 1 of Genji Dolls to form heads. Roll each skewer in one piece of white paper to form kimono and glue closed.

2. Color the kimonos with paint. Roll paper for hat into cylinder, glue closed, and glue onto prince's head. Pinch together top edges of cylinder to form peak and push down a bit.

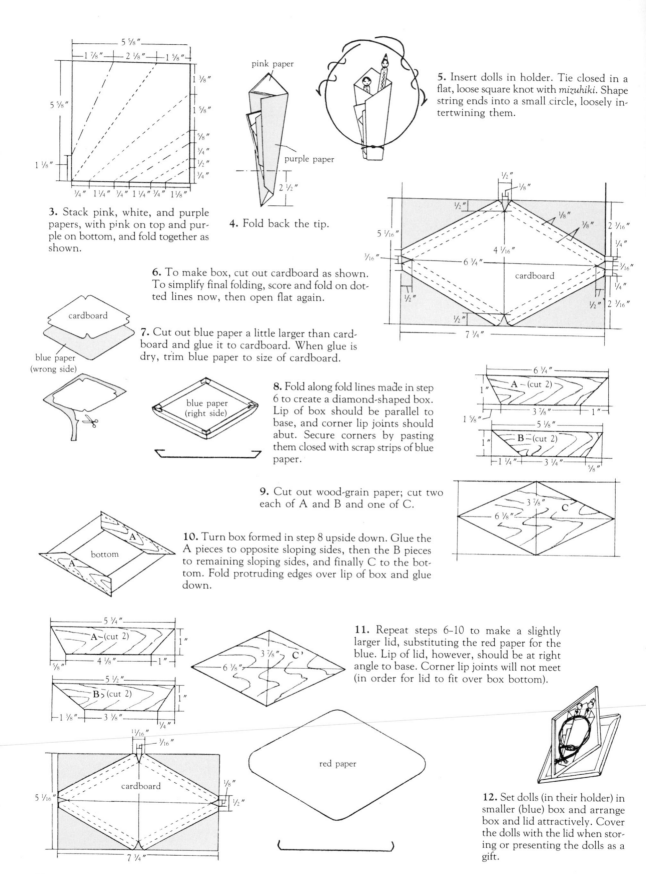

3. Stack pink, white, and purple papers, with pink on top and purple on bottom, and fold together as shown.

4. Fold back the tip.

5. Insert dolls in holder. Tie closed in a flat, loose square knot with *mizuhiki*. Shape string ends into a small circle, loosely intertwining them.

6. To make box, cut out cardboard as shown. To simplify final folding, score and fold on dotted lines now, then open flat again.

7. Cut out blue paper a little larger than cardboard and glue it to cardboard. When glue is dry, trim blue paper to size of cardboard.

8. Fold along fold lines made in step 6 to create a diamond-shaped box. Lip of box should be parallel to base, and corner lip joints should abut. Secure corners by pasting them closed with scrap strips of blue paper.

9. Cut out wood-grain paper; cut two each of A and B and one of C.

10. Turn box formed in step 8 upside down. Glue the A pieces to opposite sloping sides, then the B pieces to remaining sloping sides, and finally C to the bottom. Fold protruding edges over lip of box and glue down.

11. Repeat steps 6–10 to make a slightly larger lid, substituting the red paper for the blue. Lip of lid, however, should be at right angle to base. Corner lip joints will not meet (in order for lid to fit over box bottom).

12. Set dolls (in their holder) in smaller (blue) box and arrange box and lid attractively. Cover the dolls with the lid when storing or presenting the dolls as a gift.

planned to include seasonal motifs and sushi. The menu might center on *momo no hana zushi*—vinegared rice pressed into flower shapes and topped with pink-dyed fish to resemble peach blossoms. It would also include a soup, probably clam, symbolizing marital happiness.

The festival, and the dolls, are closely associated with the girls of the family, so much so that Girls' Day is an alternative name for the festival. In fact, a gift of *hina* dolls is customary when one's daughter gives birth to her first daughter. That granddaughter's younger sisters, however, share the dolls, which stay in the family when the daughters marry out. The department stores would have you believe that everyone must buy a full set, complete with seven-tiered stand that folds up into a compact storage box. Generally, the actual practice is to give just the emperor and empress dolls at the birth of a granddaughter, for they are the essential figures. Then the girl's family can have the pleasure of adding other dolls and fittings year after year, as they choose.

The Doll Festival is thought to descend from the Chinese custom of conducting a riverside ceremony to wash away evil on the third day of the third month. The use of dolls in the ceremony is, however, a Japanese innovation growing from a long tradition of using dolls to absorb evil influences. Combining the riverside rite to wash away malevolent influences with dolls to act as scapegoats for the humans who might otherwise be victims, the Japanese developed a custom in which special dolls—*nagashi-bina*, or dolls for washing away—are cast into the river with their burden of evil.

The dolls used as *nagashi-bina* are crude clay or paper figures. Just how such figures evolved into elegant *hina* dolls is unclear. The name *hina* itself originally referred to the paper or wooden dolls, usually a male and female pair, played with by the children of Heian times.

The Doll Festival developed into its present form in the Edo period (1603–1868). Most families with daughters, then, as now, celebrated the Doll Festival in some form or other. Whether folded paper, molded clay, bundled straw, or even painted acorns—two dolls, one female and one male, one empress and one emperor, are all it takes to create a *hina* display and the centerpiece for a celebration of daughters and a spring rite for protecting the entire household from evil influences.

The *hina* doll display: the emperor (*a*) and empress (*b*), three ladies-in-waiting (*c*), five musicians (*d*), ministers of the right (*e*) and left (*f*), mandarin orange (*g*) and cherry flowers (*h*), three pages (*i*), and miniature household items (*j*).

Cherry Blossom Viewing

Early April brings the cherry blossom. Symbol of Japan, the *sakura*, or cherry tree, represents the Japanese love of nature, the transience of beauty and life, jolly fellowship, and spring. Celebrated by poets for centuries, lovingly depicted by artists, and invariably included in postcard collections, the cherry and its cult may at first seem to be a case of hopelessly trite overkill. So much sentimental fuss over a few pink blossoms! Even the news media provide daily "cherry blossom front" reports, tracing the bloom's progress as it moves north and having experts report on the state of the buds at famous stands of cherry trees. At the same time, Japanese behavior at their famous cherry-blossom sites is far from reverent. Noise, garbage—what does that have to do with meditating on nature's beauties?

Such sour cherry attitudes may persist through the preseason media buildup, but then, suddenly, clouds of pink appear everywhere. Literature, art, and tourist guidebooks lead one to believe that cherry blossoms are as rare as they are lovely, that an expedition to one of the famous spots— Yoshino in Nara, Ueno in Tokyo—is the only way of enjoying them. But suddenly the neighborhood, the walk to the station, and the view from the train are punctuated by bursts of pink in schoolyards, vest-pocket parks, and gardens. More than one city park better known for its sports facilities than its flowers is transformed into a vision of undulating pink waves of blossoms, as lovely and improbable as a scene on an ancient screen or tea jar.

These cherry trees are almost entirely *somei yoshino*, a popular variety that matures rapidly and bears up well under the stress of the urban environment but is relatively short-lived. Its pink, five-petaled blossoms burst into bloom almost simultaneously, before the tree begins to leaf out,

producing a perfect pink cloud effect for the few days the flowers survive. True enthusiasts seek out other varieties—the earlier-blooming weeping cherry (*shidare-zakura*), the wild cherry (*yama-zakura*) in its native mountains, the extravagant double cherry (*yae-zakura*). The six families of native wild cherry trees have been multiplied into three hundred cultivated varieties, a labor attesting to the passion of gardeners for variety in blooming dates, number of petals, petal shapes, and hue. All, however, bloom only briefly, and in spring.

Enjoying the flowers as a group, with friends or co-workers, means organizing a flower-viewing party, the season's great event. Choosing a date to picnic under the trees is impossible without advance warning of the blossoms' probable debut, which fact alone is sufficient justification for the cherry blossom front reportage. Many picnickers aim for the day the flowers are expected to be in full bloom, although others prefer the promise of half-opened buds, the pathos of falling petals, or even the surreal effect of blossoms lit by lanterns, a lone street lamp, or the silvery light of the moon. The cherry's sensitivity to cold weather makes accurate prediction a tricky undertaking, but if the blossoms cooperate, everyone is ready with picnic foods and a little saké or beer for a taste of spring. The taste may be more than symbolic, for a breeze will send a blizzard of petals swirling down onto revelers and their picnics. The party is more likely to be boisterous than contemplative, the emphasis on having fun rather than appreciating the wonders of nature. The flower viewers may let go a bit and generate the noise and mountains of trash that offend others who expect a more somber, poetic response to the annual appearance of Japan's prime symbol.

According to the literary record, cherry-viewing parties began as an aristocratic pleasure in the Heian period (794–1185) and developed into monumental affairs under the shogun Toyotomi Hideyoshi in the late sixteenth century. Hideyoshi's large parties were a form of *nodate*, or outdoor tea ceremony, an elegant approach to cherry blossom viewing within the traditions of the tea ceremony. Defining the space for the party by spreading a thick cloth on the ground and setting up a large red paper umbrella, students of tea bring a portable set of tea implements and elaborate box lunches to enjoy tea, perhaps saké, sushi and other delicacies, and relaxation under the cherry blossoms.

In the following two hundred years, cherry blossom viewing as we know it today—a popular occasion for parties under the trees enjoyed by all levels of society—developed and took hold. The idea of intensifying one's appreciation of the beauty of the season in this way is so charming that you might think of adapting it to suit your area's spring glories. The point is not to reproduce the details of a *nodate* but its feeling of aesthetic appreciation. Why not sit under a dogwood or apple tree in bloom? If you like, take a bottle of wine and a simple meal—a spring salad, a loaf of good bread, and your favorite cheese or ham—to enjoy while sharing your pleasure in the season. You will be carrying on an ancient Japanese tradition.

Over the centuries a rich set of metaphors evolved around the cherry. Among the most famous themes is that linking the blossoms' fragility with death. This view of the blossoms was particularly prominent in the *Tale of the Heike*, Japan's greatest epic poem, written around the thirteenth century. Under the overall theme of transience, the tale repeatedly likens the death of young warriors to the fall of cherry petals. Perhaps because of the identification of the cherry with the warrior spirit, cherry motifs became widely used on such military equipment as sword guards and saddles.

The martial association of cherry blossoms with death must not, however, obscure the flowers' happier associations. Cherry motifs were used on many personal items because they were thought to bring good luck to the user. Perhaps that is the underlying rationale for the common use of cherry-blossom-shaped patches over holes in fragile paper sliding doors—a magical "kiss and make it well" by the cherry, or at least the improvement of an ugly spot with a beautiful form.

The fascinating possibilities of the tension between the lavish beauty of the cherry blossoms and their short lives should not obscure the primary, positive meanings of cherries—their gift of beauty and promise of spring. Nothing should be more glorious and full of promise than a wedding, where the cherry shows its uncomplicated auspicious face. *Sakura-yu*, a tea made of preserved cherry blossoms steeped in boiling water, is often served at weddings, with two linked blossoms per cup to symbolize the joining of two families by marriage. The salt-preserved blossoms unfold in the cup as they steep, symbolizing the unfolding happiness of the young couple. These are the barely opened blossoms of the double cherry, washed in diluted vinegar and salted down for about a week, and then rinsed to remove the salt before use. Cherry leaves are also preserved in salt and eaten. Their distinctive flavor adds a special bite to Japanese confections or sushi.

Weddings are not the only new beginnings set against cherry symbolism. Since the Japanese school year starts in early April, new first graders often set out on their school careers, struggling under the weight of their leather book packs, amid a benevolent pink haze of cherry blossoms. Such contact inspires some children to undertake novel approaches to celebrating the season. An aerial cherry blossom *nodate* may not be classic, but that does not keep one group of neighborhood youngsters from practicing it. Every year, with packed lunches and thermoses of tea, they head for a nearby cherry tree with low forking branches. Climbing up, they share their lunches, admire the blossoms, and chatter happily, pleased to be doing something rather special together. Thus does the true spirit of cherry blossom viewing live on.

What better way to experience the unfolding of spring than with a picnic featuring spring foods under a flowering cherry tree. The round lunch box (instructions on p. 28) contains rice balls filled with salted cherry blossoms. Other seasonal delicacies are set off with functional leaf decorations (p. 29). Grilled shrimp are served on a crane-shaped paper plate (p. 30).

A rice cake wrapped in a cherry leaf (*sakura mochi*), the quintessential spring confection, is served on a festive folded paper dish (instructions on p. 30) that echoes the pink of cherry blossoms. Tea made with preserved cherry blossoms (*sakura-yu*) is a must at weddings and other auspicious events.

LUNCH BOX

color photograph on p. 26

MATERIALS

cardboard:
2 circles, each 6 ¾″ dia.
1 circle, 5 ½″ dia.
1 strip, 2 ½″ × 21″

red paper:
2 strips, each ¾″ × 23 ½″
4 circles, each 6 ½″ dia.
1 strip, ¾″ × 18″
1 strip, 2 ½″ × 19″

white paper:
1 circle, 5 ¼″ dia.
1 strip, 3 ½″ × 21 ½″

red cord:
46″ long

NOTE: This box, modeled after traditional bentwood boxes, is suitable for carrying sandwiches, cookies, or pastry, but avoid using it with moister foods. It will last longer if lined with wax paper, doilies, or bamboo leaves before each use.

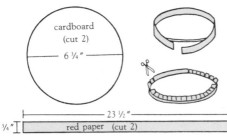

cardboard (cut 2)
6 ¼″

23 ½″
¾″ red paper (cut 2)

1. Apply glue to edge of one large cardboard circle. Wrap one 23 ½″ red paper strip around the circle, positioning edge of circle in middle of strip and gluing overlapping strip ends. Cut deeply into red paper protruding above and below, at ¼″ intervals. Glue down flaps to upper and lower surfaces of cardboard. Repeat step 1 with the other large cardboard circle.

red paper
6 ½″
(cut 4)

2. Glue red paper circles onto top and bottom of each cardboard circle.

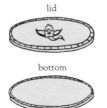

lid

bottom

3. Decorate one circle with a drawing. This circle will be lid of box, the other will be bottom of box.

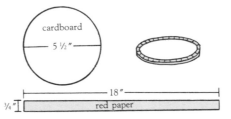

cardboard
5 ½″

18″
¾″ red paper

4. Edge smaller cardboard circle with 18″ strip of red paper, following the procedure in step 1.

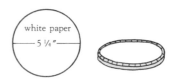

white paper
5 ¼″

5. Glue white paper circle onto center of cardboard circle prepared in step 4.

6. Center this white circle on box bottom and glue it in place, white-side up.

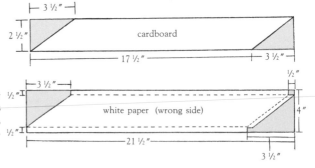

3 ½″
2 ½″   cardboard
17 ½″   3 ½″

3 ½″   ½″
½″
white paper (wrong side)   4″
½″
21 ½″
3 ½″

7. Cut the ends of strips of cardboard and white paper on diagonal, as shown. Leave ½″ flaps on three sides of paper strip. Spread glue all over one side of the paper, center cardboard on top of it, and press down firmly.

8. Fold over flaps on long sides and glue to cardboard. With white paper surface on inside, curve strip into a ring. Glue protruding paper flap to cardboard.

2 1/2" —— 19" ——

red paper

9. Spread glue on remaining strip of red paper and glue to outside of ring, overlapping strip ends.

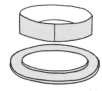

10. Glue ring to center of box bottom.

11. Put the lid on and tie with red cord.

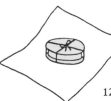

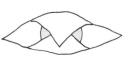

12. To carry lunch box, wrap it in a scarf or soft paper and use the knot as a handle.

LEAF DECORATIONS

color photograph on p. 26

MATERIALS

FOR BOAT: 1 leaf, about 1 1/2" × 7 1/2"

FOR KNOT: 1 leaf, about 2" × 9"

FOR DIVIDER: 1 leaf, about 3" × 12"

NOTE: Here are three functional decorations for a food display. The boat- and knot-shaped containers keep pickles and other strong-flavored foods from spilling over into neighboring tidbits. The divider helps prevent food from sticking together. Made of bamboo leaves traditionally and aspidistra leaves here, these decorations can be easily constructed from any large leaf that has no scent, doesn't discolor readily, and is nontoxic. In place of the traditional cleaver, use an X-acto knife to cut the shapes.

BOAT

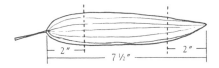

2" —— 7 1/2" —— 2"

1. Fold ends in.

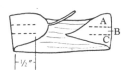

1/2"

2. Make four cuts as shown, cutting through both layers of leaf.

3. Insert loop C into loop A. Repeat for other end of leaf.

KNOT

1. Gently fold leaf tip at angle.

2. Gently fold over leaf again.

3. Bring stem end through opening as shown.

4. Pull both ends firmly to make knot-shaped container. Arrange food in pocket marked by arrow.

DIVIDER

1. Cut alternating straight and jagged lines across width of leaf.

2. Use leaf dividers with jagged edge on top. Jagged edge should just protrude above food.

SERVING PAPER (Crane)

color photograph on p. 26

MATERIALS

light blue paper: 9″ × 13″

NOTE: Place food or gifts offered to guests on elegant serving papers instead of directly on a tray or plate. The crane, a bird of good fortune, has a special place in the hearts of Japanese. Of the many ways to fold a paper crane, this is the simplest.

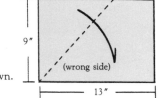

1. Fold as shown.

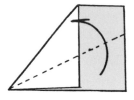

2. Fold again, aligning edges, to create a diamond.

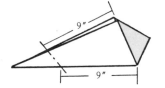

3. Fold the narrow end of the diamond up as shown.

4. Fold the tip down to form the crane's head.

SERVING PAPER (Diamond)

color photograph on p. 27

MATERIALS

thin pink paper: 9″ × 9″   **white paper:** 4″ × 4″

NOTE: The slender diamond shape folded at the left side of this serving paper is designed to resemble a *noshi*, a folded paper traditionally attached to gifts.

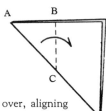

1. Fold pink paper in half into a triangle.

2. Fold left corner over, aligning with middle corner.

 **3.** Fold left edge over, aligning with center. Unfold to triangle pictured in step 2.

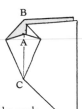

4. Hold point A straight up at right angle to fold line B-C (see step 2). Press point A down, flattening out and opening up the sides of the vertical flap to create a diamond shape.

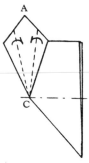

5. Fold in both sides of diamond to center line. Fold back lower point of base.

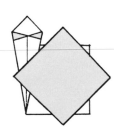

6. Decorate edges of white paper square with a red felt pen. Glue white paper on top of diamond base as shown.

Boys' Day

Boys' Day, originally called the Tango Festival, is the last of the major spring festivals. Originally celebrated on *tango*, the first (*tan*) day of the horse (*go*) in the fifth month, the festival was eventually fixed on the fifth day of May. In some years the fifth of May coincides with *rikka*, the first day of summer, but whatever the calendar says, early May is still spring, pleasantly warm and sunny but not hot.

Boys' Day (the Tango Festival) and Girl's Day (the Doll Festival) are in many ways parallel holidays, for each now is associated with the children of the family and with displays of dolls. The festivals also have similar origins in practices aimed at averting evil, practices rooted in Chinese custom but profoundly modified by centuries of Japanese use.

The Tango Festival, coming at the beginning of the busiest season of the year in an agricultural society, used the medicinal herbs mugwort (*yomogi*) and sweet flag (*shobu*, a plant resembling the iris) to cast out evil influences and put celebrators in prime condition to endure the hard work and heat of the coming summer months. In Heian times (794–1185), both those at the court and the common people hung mugwort and sweet flag from the eaves of their houses to ward off evil, a custom still widely practiced. Even today, farmhouses with thick thatched roofs may have sweet flag growing from the roof itself, providing protection year in and year out.

The sweet flag is so closely linked to this festival that the festival is also known as *shobu no sekku*, or sweet-flag festival. On this day, people often

Carp streamers on Boys' Day

Three Boys' Day dolls: (*from top*) Momotaro, hero of a folk tale, emerging from a peach (*momo*); Shoki, a demon queller; and Emperor Jimmu, the legendary first ruler of Japan, holding a bow.

drink saké with sweet-flag petals floating in it or a hot infusion of its roots. It is also the day to enjoy *shobu yu*, a steamy bath with fragrant sweet-flag leaves in it. This custom is kept alive by the public baths, which stir up business for themselves by advertising their May 5 *shobu yu*. Families without access to stands of growing sweet flag can still enjoy the ceremonial bath at home, for florists and greengrocers sell the sweet-smelling stalks for the holiday.

The slender, thick-ribbed leaves of sweet flag bear a striking resemblance to the blades of swords, and little boys enjoy dueling with them. During Japan's middle ages, a time of domination by the warrior class, the swordlike appearance of the leaves and the fact that *shobu* has a homonym meaning "respecting martial arts" were exploited to turn the Tango Festival from a general purifying ritual at the start of the farming season into a celebration of martial virtues. That was probably the point at which the festival became a boys' holiday. It became customary to encourage their nascent warlike impulses by giving them kites decorated with fierce warriors, a tradition still followed in some rural areas.

Dolls first appeared in the Tango Festival in the seventeenth century, probably in imitation of the Doll Festival for girls. The Tango Festival doll display has never been as elaborate as its model, but the display may include armor, helmet, sword, and bow as well as a few dolls of suitably military associations. Most modern-day displays consist of miniature replicas of these items.

The *koi nobori* are the most obvious difference between the Boys' Day and Girls' Day celebrations. Houses with sons display paper or cloth carp hung like streamers from tall poles so that the carp fill with wind and stand out proudly, "swimming" in the breeze. These brightly painted streamers also had their beginning in the seventeenth century, but their message is less one of martial valor than of courage in general. A carp, it is said, once swam all the way up to heaven and became a dragon. The boldly colorful paper carp urge boys to be ambitious.

Outside, brilliantly swimming on the wind, the carp streamers make Boys' Day a public celebration by the family of its having produced sons. Most commonly, one carp per son is raised on a flagpole planted in the yard or attached to the roof, accompanied by fluttering ribbons and other decorations and by two larger carp representing the parents. The eye-catching, multicolored display is best seen in smaller towns and villages, for cramped urban living has forced many families to rein in their carp.

Carp are not the only way to express pride, however. A traditional Boys' Day meal includes the felicitous *kashiwa mochi*, glutinous rice cakes stuffed with sweet bean paste and served on an oak leaf, and *chimaki*, pounded glutinous rice steamed in bamboo leaves. *Chimaki* are rolled into sharp cones so that they suggest leaves of sweet flag. It would be appropriate to serve sea bream as the main course, for this fish is synonymous with celebration in Japanese symbolism. Some of the flesh could be used in sushi, rolled up with vinegared rice in cones wrapped in bamboo leaves to suggest *chimaki* for a final variation on the Tango Festival themes. The candy manufacturers have been busy lately helping round out the celebration with *chimaki*-shaped chocolate rolled in plastic leaves and miniature chocolate helmets for the little warrior with a sweet tooth.

The Tango Festival has suffered a further indignity. Since 1948, May 5 has officially been named Children's Day, a holiday for girls as well as boys. Some families now fly carp for daughters as well as sons. Girls learn to fold paper helmets along with the boys in kindergartens and proudly take them home for the Tango display. Apart from threats to its sexual identity, the holiday is in danger of being swamped by families' efforts to travel during Golden Week, the week defined by three public holidays, of which Children's Day is the last in the series. Between the doll makers, the operators of public baths, and the confectionery companies, the Tango Festival is not likely to be forgotten, but how it will further evolve, in a society no longer agricultural or warlike that has officially embraced equality between the sexes, remains to be seen.

A formal Boys' Day display in the home alcove includes real swords and bow and arrow.

These manly eggshell figurines for Boys' Day symbolize the desire to bring up boys to be strong and healthy. Momotaro (instructions on p. 37) is the demon-quelling hero of a popular folk tale. The peach, his trademark, decorates a banner reading "Best in Japan." Benkei (p. 128), loyal companion of general Minamoto Yoshitsune, is dressed as a mountain ascetic in robe and monk's hat. Shibaraku (p. 129) is named after the famous Kabuki play *Shibaraku*, whose brave hero is known for carrying an enormous sword.

On Boys' Day, colorful carp streamers (instructions on p. 36) are hung outdoors. Indoor decorations may include such military equipment as this paper helmet (p. 36), designed to resemble the helmet of Japanese cypress that was traditionally presented to young princes at the imperial court.

CARP STREAMERS

color photograph on p. 34

MATERIALS

FOR MALE

lightweight linen: 2 pieces, each 16 ½″ × 37″
fabric dyes: navy blue, light blue, yellow, and black
wire: 11″ long   **cord:** 8 ½″ long

FOR FEMALE

lightweight linen: 2 pieces, each 12″ × 28″
fabric dyes: red-orange, burnt orange, yellow, and black
wire: 10″ long   **cord:** 8″ long

TO MAKE EITHER CARP

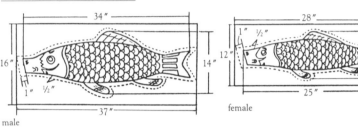

male

female

1. First draw carp on large sheet of tracing paper with a felt pen. Place one piece of linen on top of tracing-paper sketch and trace with dressmaker's chalk. Remove tracing paper. Place layers of newspaper topped by a large sheet of paper underneath the linen to absorb excess dye. Brush on dyes. Repeat with other piece of linen, reversing tracing paper, to make reverse side of carp.

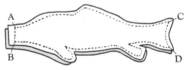

2. With wrong sides together, stitch around edges of carp. Leave sections A-B and C-D unsewn.

3. Turn carp inside out. Make a ring of wire (3 ⅛″ in diameter for male carp, 2 ¾″ for female) and insert in carp's mouth. Fold edges in and beyond ring. Stitch down edges to encase ring.

4. Sew a cord to mouth ring of carp, attaching cord ends to top and bottom of mouth, respectively.

PAPER HELMET

color photograph on p. 35

MATERIALS

cardboard: 8 ¾″ × 23″

wood-grain printed paper:
1 rectangle, 8 ¾″ × 23″
1 circle, 2 ½″ dia.

red origami paper: 6″ × 6″

5-strand gold-and-silver mizuhiki: about 36″ long

sweet flag (or iris) leaves: 3

NOTE: Wall paper or contact paper with printed wood-grain pattern may be substituted for wood-grain paper. Red paper backed with white paper may be substituted for origami paper.

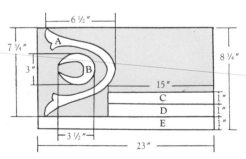

1. Glue wood-grain paper to cardboard. Cut out as shown.

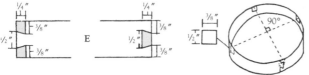

2. Make tabs on both ends of pieces C and D as shown.

3. For C, remove wood-grain paper from all shaded areas in illustration. (Carefully cut through wood-grain paper only, with an X-acto knife, then peel off paper.) For D, peel off wood-grain paper from both tabs; and remove cardboard from back of middle shaded area, leaving wood-grain paper intact.

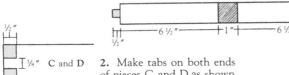

4. Cut piece E as shown and curve into a circle, wood-grain-side out, interlocking ends. Glue closed. To form notches, cut through only cardboard layer at four points shown. Carefully remove squares of cardboard, leaving wood-grain paper intact.

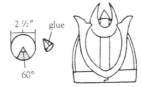

5. Overlap pieces C and D, curve into arches, fit tab ends into notches in E, and glue all joints.

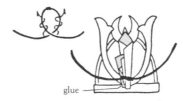

6. Cut out 60° wedge from 2 ½″ circle of wood-grain paper and curve into a cone. Glue on top where C and D overlap. Glue pieces A and B to one arch; this will be front of helmet.

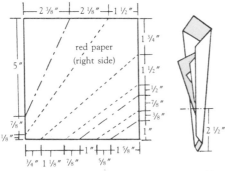

7. Fold red origami paper as shown. Fold up bottom neatly to underside and glue.

8. Glue folded origami onto front arch. Wrap *mizuhiki* strings around arch and origami, and tie in decorative flat square knot. Shape *mizuhiki* into circle, winding string ends around circle below juncture at top.

9. Insert sweet-flag leaves into origami folder.

EGGSHELL FIGURINES

color photograph on p. 35

1. To prepare eggshell, break shell at pointed end, empty out egg, rinse out inside with a water-vinegar solution, peel off thin membrane inside, and allow to dry thoroughly. Then glue torn pieces of thin paper to the inside for reinforcement. Let dry thoroughly, then trim with curved manicure scissors.

MOMOTARO

MATERIALS

body base:
1 egg
1 blank postcard (or stiff paper), 2″ wide × (circumference of egg + ½″)
stiff paper, 2″ × 2″
thin paper for reinforcing eggshell (*washi* recommended)
cotton balls
1 stone, ½″ dia.
shredded paper

kimono: (A) 3 pieces patterned paper, 1 ½″ × 6 ¼″ and (for sleeves) two of 1 ½″ × 3″

hakama: (B) 2 pieces patterned paper, 1 ½″ × 6 ¼″ and 2″ dia. circle

vest: (C) 3 pieces patterned paper, 2 ¾″ × 4″ and two of ¼″ × 1 ¾″

hair: 2 pieces black crepe paper, 1″ × 2 ¼″ and 1″ × 1″

accessories:
2 pieces white paper, 1 ½″ × 1 ½″ and ¼″ × ½″ (for hair ornaments)
white paper, 1 ½″ × 2 ¾″ (for flag)
gold paper, ½″ × ½″
bamboo skewer

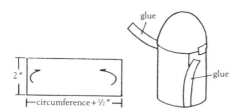

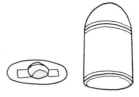

2. Glue the postcard into a cylinder. Set eggshell on cylinder, trimmed edge down, to see where the two surfaces meet. Remove eggshell to spread glue on edge of eggshell and top of cylinder, replace eggshell, and reinforce joint with a glue-backed strip of *washi*. Reinforce seam in cylinder in same way.

3. Fill eggshell with cotton batting dampened with glue. Pack cylinder with shredded paper. Trace cylinder bottom on the stiff paper square and cut out the circle.

4. Tape a stone to the circle as a weight. Glue circle to bottom edge of cylinder and reinforce by gluing a strip of *washi* around the joint.

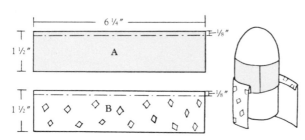

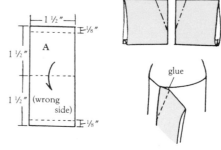

5. Fold the long strip of paper A as shown and glue to upper half of cylinder. Fold and glue on the strip of paper B, overlapping A by ⅛". Fold excess length of B under base of cylinder, gluing it down. Cut down the circle of paper B to cover the base and glue on.

6. Fold remaining two pieces of paper A as shown, for kimono sleeves. Glue bottom flaps together. Glue one sleeve to each side of kimono at triangular folded portion.

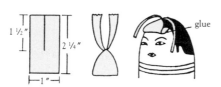

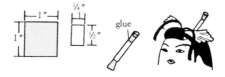

7. Paint hair and features on eggshell with paint and/or sumi ink. Make front hair out of larger piece of crepe paper, tying with black thread at 1 ½" mark as shown, and glue on. Trim thread ends.

8. Accordion-fold white paper square as shown, pinch together at center, and glue to top of head.

9. Roll up remaining square of crepe paper, gluing closed, and wrap remaining piece of white paper around it, gluing closed. Glue one end to head behind pleated decoration.

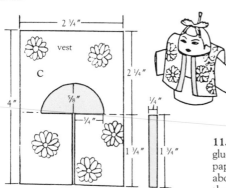

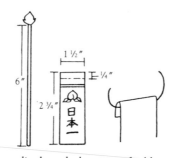

10. Cut out vest from paper C. Glue the two strips along front opening for lapels and dress figurine in vest.

11. Cut a stylized peach shape out of gold paper and glue to top of bamboo skewer. Draw a peach on white paper for flag. Lay thread along back top of flag, about ¼" from edge; fold top edge of flag over thread and glue down. Tie thread ends to top end of skewer and trim. Attach skewer to sleeve with dab of glue.

Instructions for Benkei and Shibaraku begin on p. 128.

SUMMER

early May
through
early August

For two thousand years summer was the season most intensely experienced in Japan. It was time for the backbreaking labor of transplanting and weeding rice, for planting and harvesting other crops, and for the close cooperation with neighbors without which wet rice agriculture was impossible. In the crucial season between transplanting and harvest, with enough rainfall for irrigation, enough sunlight, and typhoons timed not to flatten ripening grains, the hard work of summer would pay off in food for everyone. If not, life could be bleak indeed.

Not surprisingly, the agricultural year was punctuated with ritual to reinforce the community that made paddy rice agriculture possible and to placate the guardian diety of the fields. Today, barely a tenth of Japan's population is engaged in agriculture, and farm households earn the greater half of their income from non-agricultural occupations. The heaviest tasks have been mechanized, and the summer's work no longer requires a maximum cooperative effort to ensure community survival. Nonetheless, many traditional local festivals born of the agricultural cycle live on, even in urban areas.

Summer starts out, according to the traditional lunar calendar, in early May, then settles down to forty days and forty nights of halfhearted, misty rain beginning sometime in June. When the clouds clear, the sun reveals the lush growth brought on by the rains and starts to heat up the land in earnest. The refreshing blues and pinks of morning glories are everywhere, screening the fronts of houses, climbing telephone poles, running rampant over fences. Every child in every public first-grade class throughout Japan is required to grow a morning glory from seed, although adults may purchase potted plants at the famous morning-glory fair in Tokyo on July 7 and 8. There, more than a hundred stalls offer morning glories of all colors.

The day after the morning-glory fair ends, Tokyo begins a two-day *hozuki* (Chinese lantern plant) fair. These plants are known for the fragile, papery lanterns formed by the bright orange sepals around their red fruit. It's possible to remove the fruit without damaging the lantern and make a noisemaker: the fruit, emptied of its pulp, produces a squeak when pressed between the tongue and roof of the mouth. Generations of Japanese children have entertained themselves with their *hozuki* squeakers in the long hot summer.

How to withstand the stultifying heat and humidity is a daily concern. One way is to eat strengthening foods, particularly eel. Since Edo times it has been almost compulsory to eat grilled eel on the day of the ox (*doyo*) during the height of summer; in 1987, the great eel rush fell on July 27. It is also proper to show concern for family and friends in the heat with gifts of food that can be enjoyed cold—such as watermelon or noodles—and by sending brief notes of greeting in the period from July 15 to August 7, when summer officially ends. The gift giving, however, has been largely shifted to *chugen*, the period between July 1 and 13 when gifts are sent to relatives and those to whom one owes a debt of gratitude. Traditional *chugen* gifts are food, clothing, sweets, or lanterns for Obon.

Obon, the central summer holiday, resembles nothing so much as New Year's in its effect on the national psyche and the public transportation system. A hundred million Japanese, all determined to leave the cities for their old homes in the country, pack trains to twice capacity or worse.

The name Obon derives from *urabon*, Japanese for the Sanskrit *ullambana*, a Buddhist memorial ceremony designed to rescue souls from purgatory. Apart from having a priest visit one's home to read a sutra, however, there is little in popular Obon observances that is Buddhist in origin. Obon was accepted so wholeheartedly as a holiday after being introduced with Buddhism from China because it fit well with the native custom of welcoming back the souls of the ancestors in late summer.

Obon was celebrated according to the lunar calendar, with the main ceremonies between the thirteenth and the sixteenth of the seventh month. Now that Japan uses the Gregorian calendar, Obon's timing is rather confused. The calendar says it is celebrated from July 13 to 16, but schools are still in session then, preventing families with children from returning home. Thus, the major Obon celebration usually is a month later, closer to the lunar date, when some major corporations close for a week. Moreover, rural districts may still use the lunar calendar. Everyone does perform the ceremonies on the same day of the month, whether solar July or August or the lunar seventh month.

Obon begins with cleaning the ancestral graves on the seventh. A path may be made from grave to house to guide the spirits, with extra assistance given to the more recently deceased, who might more easily miss the way. A spirit altar is set up before the family Buddhist altar, which is closed throughout the holiday. After sundown on the thirteenth, a welcoming fire is lit. The fire not only leads the spirits home but also is felt to be where the spirits manifest themselves. Offerings of foodstuffs made of barley, already harvested if the lunar calendar applies, and seasonable vegetables are set out. Thus, the Obon observance incorporates thanksgiving for the harvest.

After sundown on the sixteenth, the spirits are sent off again with fires. A family may light a simple fire in the courtyard or float tiny rafts bearing candles down the river. The sending-off fires may also be communal—a large community boat with lanterns or a community bonfire lit on a hillside above the village. The communal approach reaches its peak in Kyoto, where a series of bonfires traces out the Chinese character for "great" on a mountainside. All exterior lighting in the city below is extinguished, and the fires are lit. When their message is glowing in the night, characters and symbols on five other mountainsides overlooking the city are lit, one after the other.

The community spirit of Obon is also seen in *bon odori*, folk dancing performed during Obon. A temporary platform for musicians and lead dancers is set up in the village square and all gather in the evening to dance in a large circle around it. The dance is thought to ease the spirits of the dead and to welcome them home.

In cities today, *bon* dancing is a popular community event that has virtually no religious significance. The fires to send off souls have become tourist attractions. And in industrialized Japan, the success or failure of the harvest is not an urgent issue for many. But families are overwhelmingly committed to the idea of going home for Obon—for a taste of the ancestral air, the family foods, a chance to meet friends from childhood and to show one's children the sites of oft-told stories. As long as Japanese care about their past, they will make Obon the heart of summer.

The Seasons of Summer

RIKKA 立夏

Summer begins with *rikka*, or the Establishment of Summer, on May 5 or 6. This seasonal marker ushers in the peak bloom month: more flowers blossom in May than in any other month.

SHOMAN 小満

May 21 or 22 brings *shoman*, or the Lesser Ripening, and continuing balmy weather. Wisteria blossoms cloak houses and arbors in a haze of purple, and the first fireflies emerge.

BOSHU 芒種

Boshu, or Grain Beards and Seeds, on June 6 or 7, means time for transplanting rice. The rainy season usually begins during *boshu*, and azaleas, gardenias, and iris come into bloom.

GESHI 夏至

The summer solstice, or *geshi*, falls on June 21 or 22. This longest day of the year passes unnoticed in Japan, for the country is shrouded in rain clouds and the sun blocked from view.

SHOSHO 小暑

Shosho, or the Lesser Heat, on July 7 or 8, is the traditional time for moving into the summer mode of living, even though the rainy season may linger. These two weeks bring the Tanabata Festival and, for those following the Gregorian calendar, Obon.

TAISHO 大暑

Japanese public schools let out for summer vacation just before *taisho*, or the Greater Heat, on July 23 or 24. The signs of summer emerge—fireworks, watermelons, festivals, cotton kimonos, and the whirring of cicadas.

Summer brings lush growth and a profusion of flowers. Some, like the popular morning glory and Chinese lantern plant, are featured at potted-plant fairs. Others, notably the iris and water lily, transform public parks and gardens, drawing crowds of admirers even in the rain and heat of summer.

dragonfly (*tonbo*)

morning glory (*asagao*)   Japanese iris (*hanashobu*)   Chinese lantern plant (*hozuki*)

water lily (*suiren*)

Heat-dulled appetites are easily stimulated by the bounty of summer and the cool presentation of year-round foods. Sweetfish in season provides needed protein, and sour pickled plums are invigorating. Chilled tofu and wheat noodles, with their smooth, cool textures, are ideal summer fare.

green plums (*aoume*)

grilled sweetfish (*ayu*)

cold tofu (*hiyayakko*)

pickled plums (*umeboshi*)

thin wheat noodles (*somen*) with dipping sauce

Flavors of Summer

Summer's heat fills the markets with luscious fruits and vegetables, but that same heat dulls appetites and enervates cooks. Accordingly, the goal of cuisine in Japan's sweltering summer becomes creation of simple dishes that tempt the palate.

Effective presentation helps, for food arranged to look cool and refreshing is more appealing. The implements used must themselves embody coolness. Thus, for instance, glass dishes—cool to the hand and eye—are reserved for summer use. Rather than serving everything on glass utensils, in a display that suggests bargains in glassware as much as coolness, try combining the icy transparency of glass with the cool colors of blue-and-white china or the natural freshness of bamboo. Another approach is to use ice itself: serve chilled soup, salad, or sashimi in a dish resting on ice or heap tofu or watermelon in a bowl with large chunks of ice.

Many of the staples of the Japanese diet, served hot in other seasons, are allowed to cool before serving in summer. Rice, for example, is consumed as room-temperature rice balls filled with bits of fish or pickles, but noodles are by far the most popular staple of summer. Cold noodles—not to be confused with cold leftover spaghetti—are part of many national cuisines. Japanese eagerly consume Chinese cold noodles in the hot months, but they also have some specialties of their own: namely, *soba* and *somen*. *Soba*, buckwheat noodles, are eaten at room temperature year-round; their firm texture and nutty flavor make a delicious base for toppings of shredded cucumber, chicken, seaweed, and sesame seeds. *Somen*, on the other hand, are exclusively a summer treat. Thin wheat noodles, softer than vermicelli, *somen* are served chilled, often on lumps of ice, with a soy-sauce-and-stock dipping sauce and garnishes of finely sliced onion and Japanese horseradish. A summer meal organized around *somen* can delight the eye and stomach.

Summer dining also offers the opportunity to enjoy the ultimate in tofu dishes: *hiyayakko*. Fresh tofu is rinsed, cut into cubes, and served chilled, perhaps on ice, with soy sauce and a range of tangy garnishes, typically grated ginger and sliced scallions. The possibilities for garnishes are boundless (watercress, for example, is an unorthodox but tasty addition), but the garnishes must not overwhelm, for the focus of *hiyayakko* is the tofu itself: its smooth texture, mild taste, and agreeable coolness.

The miracle food of summer is the innocuous-looking *ume*, or Japanese plum. These grape-sized fuzzy green balls appear on the market in June. Though inedible raw, they make wonderful sauce, jam, and wine. Plum wine (*umeshu*), actually a liqueur, is made simply by washing and drying the green plums, then steeping them in a sugar and white liquor mixture in a tightly closed container. The plums will shrivel up in a month and plump out again after about three months, at which time the liqueur may be drunk. With ice in summer or hot water in winter, this beverage is most refreshing.

Once the plum wine is in the jug, it is time to roll up your sleeves and make *umeboshi* out of the same variety of plums, now yellow and softer. *Umeboshi* are the mainstay of Japanese life. Running from an earthquake? Take ten days' supply of uncooked rice and a jar of *umeboshi*. Feeling run down? Pop an *umeboshi* in your mouth. Salted down to marinate with the leaves of the mintlike beefsteak plant (*shiso*), then sun-dried briefly, pickled plums will keep for thirty or forty years in a tightly sealed container, so strongly antibacterial are they. Thus, an *umeboshi* in the center of a ball of cooked rice—the Japanese equivalent of a peanut butter and jelly sandwich—keeps it from spoiling in hot weather. This makes *umeboshi* a godsend in summer, and their astringent taste remains one of the best remedies for heat-induced lethargy.

The Rainy Season

In May, the weather in Japan turns sunny and increasingly warm; summer is on its way, dare think the unwary. Then just when summer has set in, the stubborn Japanese climate shows its independence from calendar-imposed conventions by sneaking in an extra season. Usually in the second or third week of June, the skies become gray, rain starts falling, and the balminess of May is squelched by a nasty, damp chill. *Tsuyu*—the rainy season—has arrived.

What has happened is fairly simple: a northern maritime air mass from the Okhotsk Sea and a hot, moist tropical air mass have met over Japan and gone into equilibrium. Unfortunately, equilibrium means rain—for everybody within sixty miles of the shifting front—and clouds everywhere else in Japan. This basic weather pattern is maintained for a rainy month or so, until the balance of power between the two air masses shifts.

A month of gray skies alone is enough to bring on gloom. But *tsuyu* has worse to offer: high humidity coupled with widely ranging temperatures, so that one day feels intolerably muggy and the next penetratingly chilly. No wonder the rainy season is regarded as a depressing time, hard on everyone. It's the perfect season for going back to bed, except that the bedding is nastily soggy; the endless rain has made it impossible to air the futon or anything.

To anyone suffering through *tsuyu*, it is pointless to remark that Japan is lucky in its rainy season. It does not come at the coldest time of the year, as the rains in Taiwan do. It does not last for months, as the Southeast Asian rainy season does. And it usually does not bring floods and disease, as the monsoon rains on the Indian subcontinent do. These facts are little consolation when you discover that a pair of dress shoes, rain-soaked and foolishly put away damp, have taken advantage of the dark and warmth to metamorphose into fuzzy green bedroom slippers.

Calm is essential in dealing with *tsuyu*. Remember to stuff your shoes with newspaper to dry them, always take your umbrella, and keep life as simple as possible. This is the perfect time to while away the hours with indoor hobbies and craft projects. Do not avoid entertaining friends for the duration, but do keep arrangements simple; with everyone on edge, the rainy season is no time for elaborate parties. Students of the tea ceremony, which among other things is a study in creating a welcoming atmosphere for guests, know that the rule for *tsuyu* is simplicity and coolness. Tea-school conventions prescribe that lacquerware used at gatherings in the rainy season should be sprinkled with water and unglazed pottery dampened before use. The idea is to suggest the freshness of dew and to create a refreshing coolness to the touch. This spare, imaginative approach can help everyone look beyond the discomfort of *tsuyu* to enjoy its beauties.

The beauties are evident in paddy fields and gardens, for Japan is exploding with new growth in late June and July. The hydrangea, rather vulgar blooming under the bright sun of a Western June, is best viewed in Japan. The intense blues and purples of the clusters of blossoms seem to glow even more during a rainfall, as though the shock of falling raindrops stimulates a benign radiation. The hydrangeas of the Meigetsu-in, a temple in Kamakura, are particularly famous, but a leisurely stroll through most neighborhoods will reveal many lovely examples quietly glowing in the gloom.

Japanese irises, *hanashobu*, are also at their best during the rainy season. These relatives of the more familiar bearded iris like to be flooded at bloom time but prefer dry feet the rest of the year. Thus these irises are raised in special low beds for flooding or in boxes that can be submerged.

A bamboo forest in the rainy season

One of the best places to see irises is the Meiji Shrine in Tokyo where in 1897 the Meiji emperor had a *hanashobu* display designed for his empress. There, thousands of plants of more than a hundred varieties bloom in serpentine beds laid out to provide constantly changing vistas as one walks by.

The irises, their broad, delicate flowers held high on slim stalks, are stunningly arranged to fade from pure white to deep purple. A leisurely stroll into the enchantment of this iris garden makes one almost grateful for the rainy season.

Paper crafts, such as these traditional-style lady dolls (*anesama ningyo*), are a perfect way to pass time indoors during the rainy season. *Left to right:* The bride doll (instructions on p. 130) is dressed for her wedding day. The city girl doll (p. 51) is dressed as an unmarried girl of commoner status. The Shimada doll (p. 48) wears the Shimada hair style, the most popular style among married women of the Edo period.

LADY DOLLS

color photograph on p. 47

SHIMADA DOLL

MATERIALS

head:
2 pieces white paper (*washi* recommended), 10″ × 11 ½″ and (for neck lining) 1″ × 10″
cotton batting

hair ornaments:
3 strips silver paper, ⅛″ × 1″ and two of ⅛″ × 4″
2 strips stiff yellow paper, ½″ × 1″ and ¼″ × 1 ½″
1 circle stiff red paper, ¼″ dia.
purple tie-dyed silk (or any lightweight textured fabric, such as crepe), ½″ × 4″

underkimono: 2 pieces light pink paper, 4 ¼″ × 8 ½″ and (for collar) 1″ × 3 ¾″

kimono:
light blue patterned paper, 4 ½″ × 11″
lavender paper, 4 ½″ × 9″ (for lining)

obi (sash):
white paper, 1″ × 3 ½″
2 pieces blue patterned paper, 2 ¾″ × 3 ¾″ (for front) and 4″ × 6 ½″ (for back)
light green paper, ⅛″ × 3 ½″ (for obi cord)

1. Cut white paper for hair and face as shown.

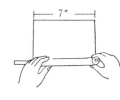

2. To make coil, lightly crumple paper, roll it loosely around chopstick (or popsicle stick), then push ends toward middle, wrinkling paper. Carefully unwind paper and smooth out a bit. Then roll on chopstick again and repeat process four or five times until paper is covered with fine wrinkles.

3. With coil on chopstick wrinkled to 4 ¾″ width, unwind a 4″ tail of paper. Pull out chopstick, then thread an 8″ white string or paper twist (see p. 56) through it. (Paper twist may be substituted for string throughout Lady Doll instructions.)

4. With tail hanging down the inside, bring ends of paper roll together and tie the string.

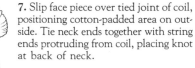

5. Fold white paper for neck lining in thirds lengthwise, then in half at middle.

6. Fold face paper (step 1) in thirds lengthwise, then open out. Place a pinch of cotton ball and then neck lining on face paper as shown. Refold face paper around lining and fold in half at middle.

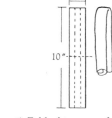

7. Slip face piece over tied joint of coil, positioning cotton-padded area on outside. Tie neck ends together with string ends protruding from coil, placing knot at back of neck.

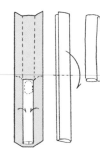

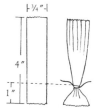

8. Prepare paper for front hair as in step 2. Wrinkle up until ¾″ wide. Carefully unroll from chopstick, flattening slightly. Tie with string 1″ from one end.

9. Glue short end of front hair across top of face piece as shown. Insert long end into center of coil ring.

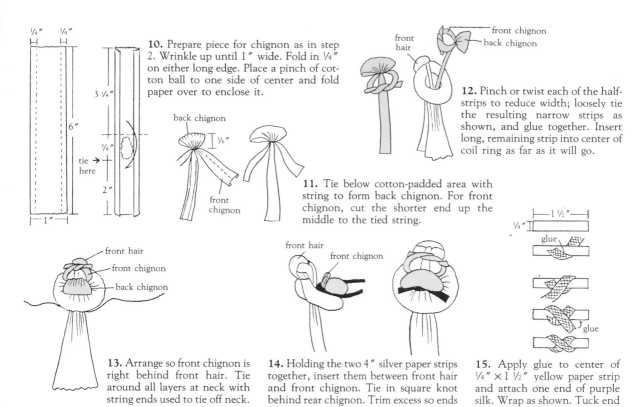

10. Prepare piece for chignon as in step 2. Wrinkle up until 1″ wide. Fold in ¼″ on either long edge. Place a pinch of cotton ball to one side of center and fold paper over to enclose it.

12. Pinch or twist each of the half-strips to reduce width; loosely tie the resulting narrow strips as shown, and glue together. Insert long, remaining strip into center of coil ring as far as it will go.

11. Tie below cotton-padded area with string to form back chignon. For front chignon, cut the shorter end up the middle to the tied string.

13. Arrange so front chignon is right behind front hair. Tie around all layers at neck with string ends used to tie off neck.

14. Holding the two 4″ silver paper strips together, insert them between front hair and front chignon. Tie in square knot behind rear chignon. Trim excess so ends fall within width of coil.

15. Apply glue to center of ¼″ × 1 ½″ yellow paper strip and attach one end of purple silk. Wrap as shown. Tuck end under in back and glue.

16. Place decoration from step 15 at center of circle made by front chignon and glue down.

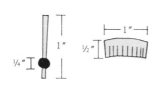

17. For comb, make cuts in ½″ × 1″ yellow paper, as shown. Glue red circle to remaining strip of silver paper to make a beaded hairpin.

18. Spread glue on both sides of comb teeth and insert teeth between front hair and front chignon. Glue hairpin beneath back chignon, as shown, to complete hairdo.

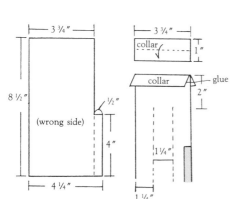

19. Cut out underkimono and fold edge as shown. Fold collar piece and glue around top edge of underkimono. Fold along lines indicated and unfold.

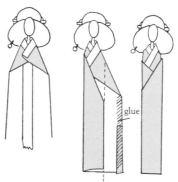

20. Center doll's head on top edge of underkimono. Fold down collar edge at an angle, (doll's) right side first, then left side. Fold kimono sides in, right side first, along fold lines made in step 19 so that width at hemline is 1 ¼″. Apply glue along inside left front edge and glue down.

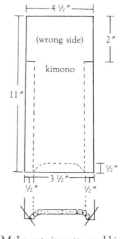

21. Make cuts in patterned kimono paper as shown. To make curve along bottom edge, make cuts in edge at sharp curves, fold up along dotted line, and glue down flaps. Cut off bottom corners at an angle. Fold in sides; then unfold.

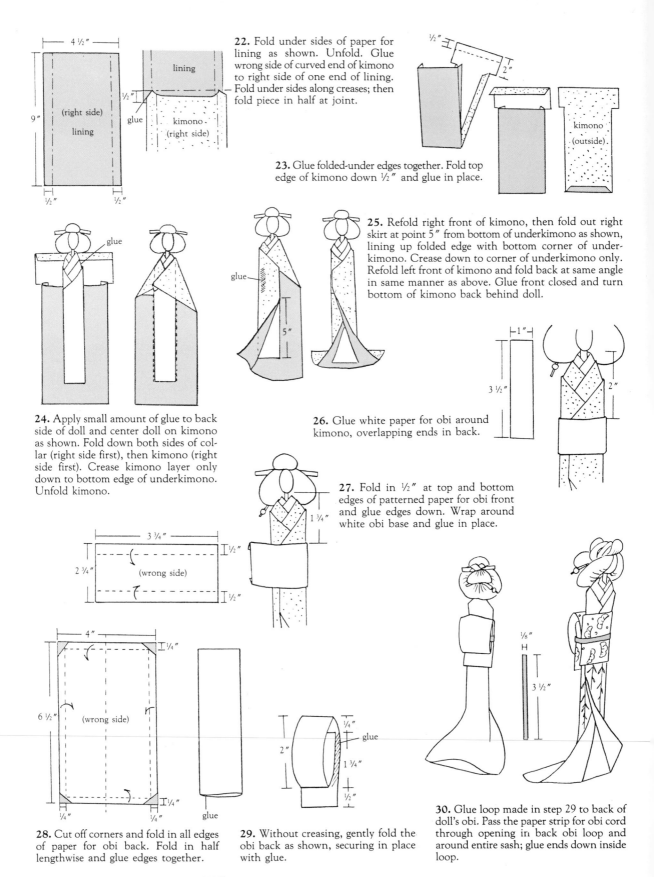

22. Fold under sides of paper for lining as shown. Unfold. Glue wrong side of curved end of kimono to right side of one end of lining. Fold under sides along creases; then fold piece in half at joint.

23. Glue folded-under edges together. Fold top edge of kimono down ½" and glue in place.

25. Refold right front of kimono, then fold out right skirt at point 5" from bottom of underkimono as shown, lining up folded edge with bottom corner of under-kimono. Crease down to corner of underkimono only. Refold left front of kimono and fold back at same angle in same manner as above. Glue front closed and turn bottom of kimono back behind doll.

24. Apply small amount of glue to back side of doll and center doll on kimono as shown. Fold down both sides of collar (right side first), then kimono (right side first). Crease kimono layer only down to bottom edge of underkimono. Unfold kimono.

26. Glue white paper for obi around kimono, overlapping ends in back.

27. Fold in ½" at top and bottom edges of patterned paper for obi front and glue edges down. Wrap around white obi base and glue in place.

28. Cut off corners and fold in all edges of paper for obi back. Fold in half lengthwise and glue edges together.

29. Without creasing, gently fold the obi back as shown, securing in place with glue.

30. Glue loop made in step 29 to back of doll's obi. Pass the paper strip for obi cord through opening in back obi loop and around entire sash; glue ends down inside loop.

CITY GIRL DOLL

MATERIALS

head: same as for Shimada Doll (p. 48)

hair ornaments:
pink fabric, ⅛″ × 1 ½″
single-strand gold *mizuhiki*, 10″ long
red tie-dyed silk (or any lightweight textured fabric, such as crepe), ¾″ × 2″
4 strips silver paper, each ¼″ × ¾″
2 strips red paper, each ¼″ × ¾″
red silk thread, 60″ long (cut into thirty 2″ pieces)
stiff silver paper, 1″ × 1 ¼″
fine wire, ½″ long

underkimono: pink patterned paper, 4 ¼″ × 8 ½″ and (for collar) 1″ × 3 ¾″

kimono:
lavender patterned paper, 4 ½″ × 11″
light pink paper, 4 ½″ × 9″ (for lining)

obi (sash):
white paper, 1″ × 3 ½″
2 pieces light pink patterned paper, 2 ¾″ × 3 ¾″ (for front) and 1″ × 2 ½″ (for knot)
rose pink patterned paper, 3 ½″ × 10 ¼″ (for bow)
rose pink paper, ⅛″ × 3 ½″ (for obi cord)

NOTE: The obi can be tied in a remarkable number of ways, each with its own suggestion of sophistication, playfulness, youth, maturity, or fashion. Designs may be dyed or woven along the length of the swath of fabric to produce, when tied, such effects as that of the City Girl's obi. The various shades of pink in her obi were, in fact, all obtained from one sheet of gradated, patterned paper. The shades are specified separately here so substitutions can be made for the Japanese paper.

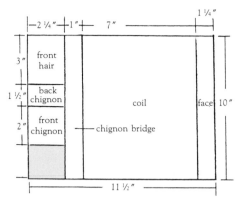

1. Cut white paper for hair and face as shown. Following steps 2–7 for Shimada Doll, make hair coil and face piece.

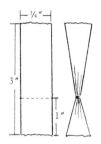

2. Wrinkle paper for front hair to width shown and tie with string 1″ from bottom.

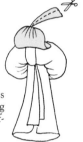

3. Glue short end of front hair across top of face piece as shown. Cut the long end widthwise in two. Pinch each half-strip to reduce width.

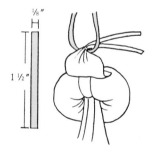

4. Tie strip of pink fabric in square knot around string on front hair.

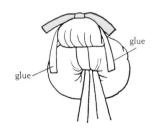

5. Cut fabric ends to even lengths. Bring the two front-hair strips to either side of doll's face and glue to coil as shown.

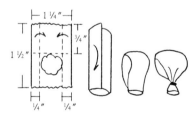

6. Wrinkle piece for back chignon to 1 ¼″ width. Place a pinch of cotton ball as shown, fold in sides, fold piece in half, and tie under the cotton-padded area.

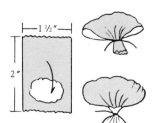

7. Make front chignon in similar manner, but wrinkle paper to 1 ½″ width and don't fold in sides. Overlap the tied joints of the two chignons and tie together with string as shown.

8. Bend gold *mizuhiki* into a figure 8 and tie with string to hold as shown. Fold the chignon bridge three times lengthwise.

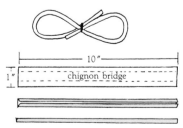

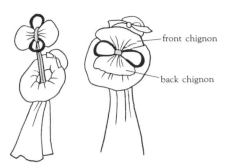

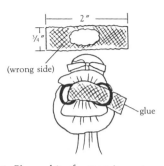

front chignon

back chignon

2″

¼″

(wrong side)

glue

9. Thread folded chignon bridge through figure 8 of gold *mizuhiki* and around joint between front and back chignons. Tie string around ends underneath chignons.

10. Insert assembly from step 9 into hole in center of coil.

11. Place a bit of cotton in center of wrong side of red silk strip. Fold under long edges and lay strip, right-side up, over bridge between chignons. Pass silk ends through loops of *mizuhiki*, then overlap and glue ends together underneath back chignon.

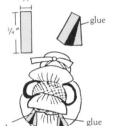

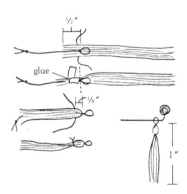

¼″

¾″

glue

glue

glue

glue

12. To make two fan shapes, glue together ends of silver and red paper strips (two silver and one red per fan). Glue fan ends under back chignon as shown.

13. Cut out a comb from stiff silver paper. Glue a bit of red silk to one side (the front), then glue comb teeth between front hair and front chignon.

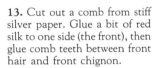

1 ¼″

1″

14. Make a tiny loop in end of 6″ piece of red thread. Knot other end. Stack the thirty 2″ threads neatly; place thread loop on top at one end of stack. Wrap a ⅛″ wide strip of scrap paper around all threads at base of loop and glue closed. Bring threads over paper collar, concealing it, and tie with a short length of thread ⅛″ from base of loop to make tassel. Make a tiny ball of cotton, glue to end of wire piece, and glue a scrap of red silk around it. Run the wire through loop in tassel, bend up ball end of wire at right angle, and glue wire, as a hairpin, under right edge of front chignon.

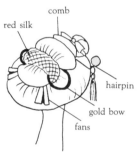

comb

red silk

hairpin

gold bow

fans

½″

glue

⅛″

1″

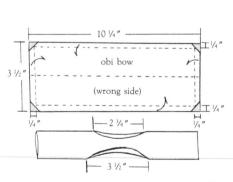

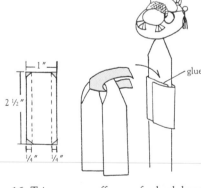

10 ¼″

¼″

¼″

¼″

¼″

obi bow

(wrong side)

3 ½″

2 ¼″

3 ½″

1″

2 ½″

¼″

¼″

glue

15. Follow steps 19–27 for Shimada Doll to make kimono and obi front. Then trim corners off obi bow as shown. Fold in edges, then fold in half lengthwise and glue edges together. Pinch in middle as shown.

16. Trim corners off paper for back knot and fold in edges. Fold knot around obi bow and insert knot ends between obi and kimono (on back of doll). Glue in place. Wrap paper strip for obi cord around obi and glue ends together in back.

Instructions for Bride Doll begin on p. 130.

The Tanabata Festival

A green branch gaily hung with colorful ornaments—is it Christmas in July? No, July 7 is the Tanabata Festival, unique among Japanese holidays for its theme of romantic love. The story now celebrated at Tanabata is the Chinese tale of the Heavenly Weaver and the Cow Herd. The Weaver, the daughter of a Chinese deity, wove cloth for the heavenly deities. On a visit to earth, she fell in love with a human, the Cow Herd, married him and bore him children, neglecting her loom for several years. The Queen of Heaven, wanting new clothes, was furious at the Weaver's dereliction of duty. In revenge, she turned the lovers into stars (the Weaver is Vega, the Cow Herd Altair) and separated them with a heavenly river, the Milky Way. Once a year, however, they draw near the opposite banks of the river, and all the magpies in the world gather there to form a winged bridge so the lovers can meet.

To celebrate the festival, Japanese families cut (or, in cities, buy) a bamboo branch and make paper ornaments for it. Wishes, preferably expressed in poems, are written on colorful paper strips and hung on the branch. Appropriately, the aspirations are usually romantic. The following evening the family casts the bamboo branch, poems, and decorations into a river or, alternatively, burns them all.

When the Chinese legend became widely known in Japan, it was incorporated into the Obon festival. (The name Tanabata comes from Tanabatatsume, a maiden who wove garments for deities to wear at Obon.) In the modified version of the tale, the Weaver and Cow Herd met on lunar double seven if the sky was clear. A cloudy sky kept them apart, and rain was their tears of frustration. After enjoying their brief time together, weather permitting, the two stellar deities performed a purification ceremony, thus preparing the way for Obon. Today, since Tanabata is usually celebrated in accordance with the Gregorian calendar and Obon a month later, the relationship between the two events has been lost. Moreover, on July 7 most of Japan is still shrouded in rain clouds so that, under the new calendar, the Weaver and Cow Herd are doomed, year after year, not to meet.

During the Edo period, merchants began putting up gay decorations to attract customers during the Tanabata season, taking the family observance and turning it into a public celebration. The result was a merchants' festival, a cheerful occasion for the townspeople to mingle, enjoy the decorations, and spend money.

Something of that merchants' festival survives in the two best-known public Tanabata celebrations—those in Sendai, a city in the northeast, and Hiratsuka, a town south of Tokyo. Both Hiratsuka and Sendai celebrate Tanabata on August 7, which is closer to the old lunar calendar date. Sendai's festival, which draws two million visitors, starts off with fireworks and *bon* dancing, followed by parades down the main streets, which are lined with long, arching bamboo poles hung with lavish decorations that flutter in the evening breeze. The clever paper and bamboo ornaments create an exotic atmosphere for the tourists who thread their way through the fluttering forest of Tanabata symbols. The colorful long streamers symbolize the Weaver's threads. Other decorations are wishes: a kimono implies the traditional wish for skill in needlework; a poem, for calligraphic skill; a crane, for long life.

Both family and merchant Tanabata celebrations are now far removed from the original purification ceremony. Yet, whether one enjoys a quiet time with the family, making decorations and writing down wishes, or joins the excitement and throngs at one of the big Tanabata Festivals, the day does offer a measure of refreshment and psychological escape from the summer doldrums.

The association of the Tanabata Festival with the "river of heaven" (the Milky Way) has led to such water-related decorations as this boat with net and fish, all cut from a single sheet of paper (instructions on p. 56). The poem strip (p. 56) carries a wish in verse. The paper kimono decoration (p. 57) symbolizes a wish for improved weaving and sewing skills.

The shadow lantern (instructions on p. 58) has been a summer pleasure in Japan for several centuries. Inside the lantern is a cylinder of paper with decorative cutout shapes. When the candle in the cylinder is lit, the cylinder turns, sending shadow pictures racing around the lantern walls.

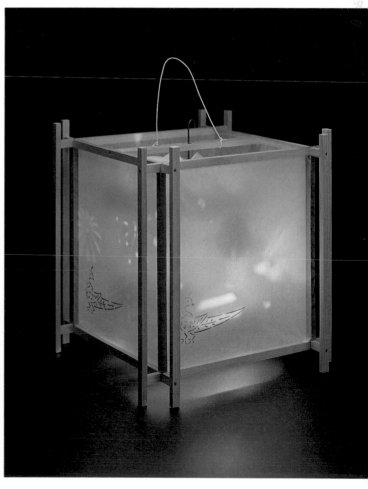

FISHING BOAT

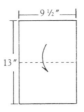

color photograph on p. 54

MATERIALS

white paper: $9\frac{1}{2}'' \times 13''$

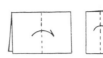

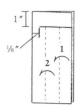

1. Fold as shown.

2. Cut across $1''$ from top stopping $\frac{1}{8}''$ from folded edge. Fold lengthwise beneath cut in order shown.

3. Cut in from alternate sides; the closer together the cuts, the better. Leave the bottom $1\frac{5}{8}''$ uncut.

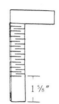

4. Unfold the two folds made in step 2. Cut out a fish shape, leaving mouth attached to net.

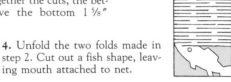

6. Unfold one more fold. Fold down corner cut in step 5, and fold over again. Undo both folds and open up corner pouch as shown, flattening out to make isosceles triangle.

7. Bring lower corners together and glue closed to make end of boat. Repeat steps 6–7 for other corner.

5. Unfold one more fold. Make cuts shown.

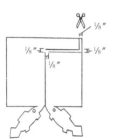

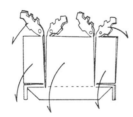

8. Turn entire paper 180° so fish are at top. Carefully unfold remaining folded portion (fish and net) and hang over sides of boat.

9. Gently stretch out net. Hang up boat and net by loops cut out at either end of boat.

POEM STRIPS

color photograph on p. 54

MATERIALS

white paper (strong washi recommended): 3 strips, each $\frac{1}{2}'' \times 10''$

paper with printed designs:
3 strips, $1\frac{3}{4}'' \times 6''$, $1\frac{1}{2}'' \times 8''$, and $1\frac{3}{4}'' \times 12''$

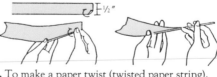

1. To make a paper twist (twisted paper string), grasp a white paper strip in both hands. Starting at one corner, twist strip clockwise between thumb and first finger of right hand, moving slowly down strip.

2. Poke hole toward top of each printed strip just big enough for paper twist to pass through. To keep paper twist from falling out, untwist and flatten one end after passing it through hole. Write poems or wishes on the poem strips and tie to branch with other end of paper twist.

PAPER KIMONO

MATERIALS

paper with printed design: 5 ¾″ × 12 ½″

paper twist (see Poem Strips, step 1) or any string

bamboo skewer: 3″ to 5″ long

color photograph on p. 54

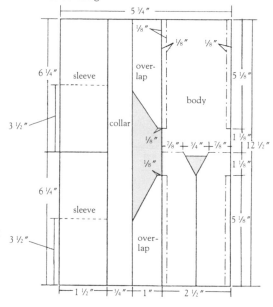

1. Cut out kimono pieces as shown, snipping body piece at points indicated.

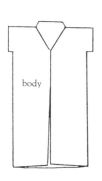

2. Fold under side edges of body piece. Fold piece at shoulders. Glue folded edge seams together.

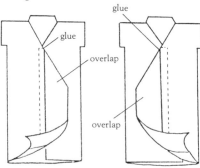

3. Glue overlaps to front opening of body front. Place left front side over right side.

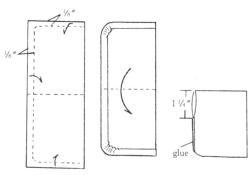

4. Fold under three edges of each sleeve, rounding corners by gathering folded seam allowance. Fold in half and glue folded edges closed, leaving 1 ¼″ armhole opening unglued.

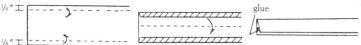

5. Fold long edges of collar in, then fold in half lengthwise.

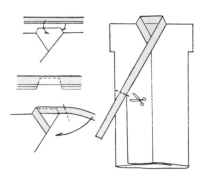

6. Spread glue on inside flaps of collar and glue together, centering over protruding tab at top of body piece. Spread glue on edges of front neck opening, fold collar ends over, and glue collar down to neck opening. Cut off protruding collar ends.

7. Glue sleeves around sleeve tabs extending from body piece. Tie paper twist to center of skewer. Hang kimono on bamboo skewer, with left side overlapping right, and tie other end of string to branch.

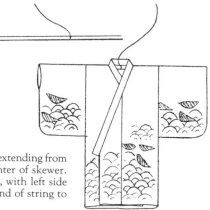

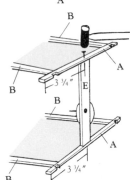

SHADOW LANTERN

color photograph on p. 55

MATERIALS

wood:
¼" × ¼" : (A) 8 sticks, each 7 ½" long
 (B) 4 sticks, each 6 ½" long
 (C) 8 sticks, each 8 ⅜" long
¼" × ⅝" : (D) 1 stick, 6 ½" long (for top crossbar)
 (E) 1 stick, 6" long (for base crossbar)

paper:
4 sheets tracing paper, each 6 ⅜" × 6 ⅞"
3 pieces stiff white paper, 5 ½" × 5 ½" and two of
 ½" × 15 ½"
1 sheet white paper, 5" × 15 ½"
cellophane paper in attractive colors

thin sheet aluminum:
1 circle, 1 ½" dia.
1 circle, 1 ⅛" dia.

nails:
26 thin nails, each ½" long
1 nail, 2" long

small clamshell

candle: ¾" dia. × 3"

wire:
1 piece, 1/16" dia. × 8 ½"
 thin wire, a few inches

sturdy string: 23" long

rubber: 1 circle, about 1" dia. × ¼" thick (any shape eraser
 may be substituted)

1. Cut notches in both ends of all A sticks as shown.

2. Combine four A sticks and four B sticks into two frames like that shown. Glue at contact points.

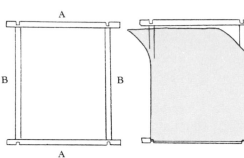

3. Glue a sheet of tracing paper tautly to each of the two frames. Cut out notches where paper covers A stick notches. (Cut out notches wherever tracing paper covers wood notches in later steps as well.)

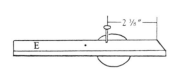

4. Mark center of piece E on one broad side. Nail on 1 ½" circle of aluminum with 2" nail at point shown, starting nailhole with an awl to prevent wood from splitting. Nail will extend out other side to form candleholder. Be sure aluminum does not cover midpoint of E.

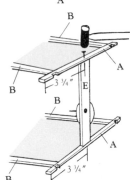

5. Glue one end of E to midpoint of A piece in one frame, with tracing paper on side facing E. Secure with thin nail. Glue and nail other end of E to A piece in other frame in like manner.

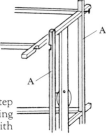

6. Fit remaining four A sticks from step 1 on frame made in step 5, interlocking notches. Glue joints, then secure with nails.

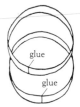

7. Curve each stiff paper strip into a ring and glue ends together, overlapping by ⅜".

8. Cut out decorative shapes in sheet of white paper. Glue pieces of colored cellophane paper behind each cutout, varying colors as you like.

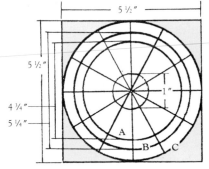

9. On the stiff-paper square draw concentric circles with the diameters shown. Draw lines dividing circle into 12 equal parts.

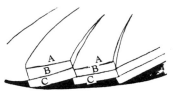

10. From outside edge, cut along lines up to innermost 1″ diameter circle to make vanes. Place vane wheel over a ring made in step 7. Bend end of one vane over outside edge of ring, gluing it down at an angle so that A line aligns with ring edge at one side of vane and C line aligns with ring edge at other side of vane. Repeat for each vane, slightly overlapping corners as you go.

11. Apply glue to outside edge of circle made in step 10, and glue the paper with cutouts from step 8 around it to form a cylinder, with cellophane side on inside. Glue overlapping edges of cylinder together. Glue other ring made in step 7 to bottom inside edge of cylinder.

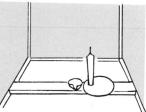

12. Glue tracing paper to inside of open sides of one frame from step 6. Glue a shell to midpoint of E and spear a candle on protruding nail.

13. Drill ⅛″ diameter holes in center of D stick and 1 ¼″ on either side of center. Side holes are slightly offset to prevent splitting in wood. To make carrying handle, tie a 9″ piece of sturdy string between the side holes. Cut shallow grooves to hold string ties attached to A sticks (see step 16) at points shown.

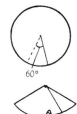

14. At center of 1 ⅛″ aluminum circle, make a hole for wire to pass through. Cut from edge to center hole and curve into cone. To secure, snip through top layer over bottom corner and bend up both corners together with pliers. This safety shield is for dissipating concentrated heat directly over candle.

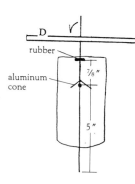

15. Sharpen end of 8 ½″ wire with file and poke down through center top of cylinder made in step 11 and then through the rubber piece, leaving 1 ⅞″ of wire sticking out above top of rubber. Thread aluminum cone on wire and position it ⅞″ below rubber by wrapping fine wire around wire shaft at the appropriate spot. Pass top end of wire shaft through midpoint hole of D and bend tip back so wire cannot slip out of hole.

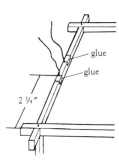

16. Glue on two 3 ½″ lengths of string to one top A stick as shown. Reinforce with glued-on paper strips. (These strings will hold the crossbar D in place, and can be untied to remove D and facilitate lighting of candle.) Repeat for other top A stick.

17. Glue the C pieces to protruding ends of A sticks at corners of lantern. Secure with thin nails.

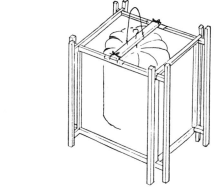

18. Glue tracing paper to remaining side of lantern from inside. Lower the cylinder suspended from crossbar D (step 15) into lantern so that bottom of wire rests on shell. Tie crossbar in place with strings. You may wish to paint simple designs on tracing paper walls so lantern will be attractive even when not lit.

19. Light the candle. (To do so, untie D and lift up, removing cylinder assembly; light candle; carefully lower cylinder over flame and tie D back in place.) Convection currents will turn cylinder clockwise (if vanes are glued in manner explained above) and send colorful moving shapes dancing around walls of lantern. Do not leave lit lantern unattended.

Summary Festivals

Merchants in Japan have appropriated the word *matsuri* (festival) to mean a discount sale, whether of beef or Buddhist altars, but to most people a *matsuri* is a local festival celebrating the community and the deity enshrined in the local Shinto shrine. The heart of any *matsuri* is a symbolic act through which participants enter into active communication with the deities and into communion with other participants. Communion with the gods requires formal offerings, while that with fellow townspeople entails a release from everyday conventions. It is this combination of formality and informality that generates the liminal state characteristic of these festivals, a state that, at least momentarily, puts the oppressive summer heat out of mind.

Name a *matsuri*, you ask a Japanese friend, and the answer is likely to be one of the major urban summer festivals that attract thousands of tourists and residents each year. The first of these is the Kanda *matsuri*, celebrated between May 13 and 18 in the Kanda district of Tokyo. The Kanda Festival is sponsored by the Kanda Shrine (also known as Kanda Myojin), which is now dedicated to Onamuchi no Mikoto and Sukunahiko no Mikoto, two deities involved in the pacification of the Japanese archipelago in mythic times. In earlier times, the shrine was associated with propitiating the spirit of the rebel Taira no Masakado.

On the Saturday before May 15, a solemn ritual is performed at Kanda Shrine to transfer the spirits of Onamuchi no Mikoto and Taira no Masakado from their manifestation in the shrine to the *mikoshi* that will be paraded through the district during the festival. *Mikoshi*, which play an important role in most festivals, are portable Shinto shrines, usually quite ornate, with fantastic roofs often crowned by gilded phoenixes. They rest on two long horizontal poles, by which they are borne on the shoulders of parishioners during the festival. The day after the ritual occurs, the *mikoshi* are carried to the shrine. The wild careening of the *mikoshi* as it enters the shrine precincts is the high point of the festival. The impassioned *mikoshi* bearers dance toward the shrine building, a whirlpool of divine madness swirling through the precincts, and then quietly they halt before the shrine and bow to the gods. After this moment of silence, the *mikoshi* again surges out to circulate through the town.

From May 16 through 18, the *mikoshi* proceeds through an extensive swath of downtown Tokyo—the Nihonbashi and Kanda districts, which are regarded as under the protection of the Kanda Shrine deities. The *mikoshi*'s procession through the neighborhoods represents the gods visiting their parishioners and extending their protection through the coming year. Residents prepare by cleaning house thoroughly, hanging lanterns outside, and putting up decorations to welcome the gods.

In addition to the *mikoshi*, the Kanda Festival includes floats, wagons filled with dancers, and acres of temporary stalls selling every sort of snack, trinket, or toy imaginable and offering an array of ingenious games. Some sell the sweet saké (*amazake*) and special fermented soybeans (*shibazaki natto*) associated with the festival. To set out of an evening in a cheerful cotton kimono to shop all the stalls, listen to the musicians, and perhaps pay one's respects at the shrine makes an exciting break for the hardworking resident of downtown Tokyo.

Hard on the heels of the Kanda Festival comes the Sanja Festival, a celebration by Asakusa Shrine (also known as Sanja Myojin), located beside Tokyo's popular Asakusa Kannon Temple. Anyone wishing to experience sensory overload is urged to head for Asakusa on the Saturday and Sunday nearest May 17 and 18. A pack of some one hundred *mikoshi* prowl the narrow streets. Geisha and

others dance to traditional music. The cacophony, the press of people, and the colorful shops and stalls compound the chaos. Those who are not parishioners of the shrine might wish to return on a quieter day to admire the Edo-period shrine building and explore the shops that line the walkway leading to the temple.

If the major Tokyo festivals are vigorous and bustling events, Kyoto's Gion Festival is sedate and elegant, as it should be in Japan's ancient capital. Like the Kanda Festival, the Gion Festival is a propitiary event designed to avert plague and pestilence from the city. It dates back to 869, when an epidemic sweeping Kyoto was traced to a curse by the deity Gozu Tenno. Sixty-six tall spears were erected to him in the imperial park and prayers were offered. Later Gozu Tenno was enshrined in the Yasaka Shrine, also known as Gion-san, and the festival became its responsibility. Now the Gion Festival means summer to Kyoto dwellers.

The festival begins on July 1, but the highlights fall on July 16 and 17. On the night of the sixteenth, towering spear-laden floats (*yamaboko*) are hung with lanterns, and many who come to admire them also take advantage of a special tradition of the district: old, prosperous families open their windows to let passers-by see the screens and other art objects that they have collected over the generations. The families also take the opportunity to invite friends in to enjoy a closer view of their treasures and savor a meal built around the chief festival food, conger eel.

The following day, the thirty-one *yamaboko*, gorgeously decorated and carrying musicians, roll out to parade the streets. Smaller shoulder-borne floats also circulate the city. Participants may carry a branch of the sacred *sakaki* tree or a *chimaki* (rice wrapped in a bamboo leaf) tucked into their sashes for purification and protection during the serious work of the festival. *Chimaki* sold by the floats also bear inscriptions promising protection against sickness through the generations.

All of Japan's major summer festivals are blatantly advertised as tourist attractions and draw thousands of visitors who have no relation to the shrine holding the festival. Commercialization does not mean, however, that the core of meaning has been lost. These festivals have been maintained by the efforts of local people who believe that something more than tourist revenues would be lost if the portable shrines or floats did not circulate through their streets. Certainly, no one who has experienced the special blend of community spirit and excitement can deny the magic of a Japanese summer festival.

Creating Coolness

Japan's short, muggy summer is a challenge to the idea of living in harmony with the seasons. Spring and fall, with their mild weather, make appreciating the changing natural world almost too easy. In summer, however, the exhausting glare of the sun and the high humidity rob one of the energy to find ways to enjoy or even tolerate summer. Now that air conditioning is widely available, turning it on, closing the curtains, and pretending that there is no such thing as summer is a seductively easy response. Denial, unfortunately, does not improve the weather outside, and stepping from a refrigerated room makes the heat and humidity even harder to bear. Relying only on air conditioning to make the summer tolerable leads to hiding indoors—and all the sights, scents, and sounds of summer pass unnoticed.

Not long ago, when air conditioning was unknown, we all had to face up to summer, especially in Japan where the traditional architecture made an active response to the challenge of summer a necessity. Houses and apartments are still built, as much as possible, with sliding glass doors on the southern side to trap the sun's light and warmth. In summer, such passive solar heating creates an interior inferno, unless steps are taken to counteract the heat. The Japanese approach is to redecorate the home interior for summer, not only to keep the indoor temperature down but also to create a display of coolness.

The first step is to block the sunlight. *Shoji*, sliding doors of translucent paper, are taken out and replaced with *sudo*, frames holding horizontal strips of split bamboo that filter the light while permitting a breeze to pass through. *Sudare*, bamboo blinds, are hung outside windows and doors to provide further protection from the sun. Shutting out the light entirely with opaque blinds might be more effective, but at the cost of shutting out the welcome aspects of summer: the refreshing breezes that stir at nightfall, the sounds of insects and birds, the filtered green of summer's luxuriant gardens.

Doorway curtains (*noren*) hanging at the entrance to the house or kitchen or living room are also renewed for summer. Translucent, yet crisp, summer fabrics replace the usual indigo-dyed heavy cotton. Floor cushions should be recovered in summery fabrics. Linen covers in blue and white, for instance, are comfortable to sit on while providing a cool color accent as well. Cushions covered with woven reeds or circles of braided straw are also available for summer use.

Bedding, too, changes in the summer, and not just by using thinner covers. A woven reed mat (*negoza*) spread directly under the body promotes a good night's sleep on the hottest nights with its smooth surface that wicks away perspiration. Sleeping on a summer pillow of rattan or bamboo is a skill not readily acquired, but the principle behind it—permitting air to flow about the head—is sound.

When the whole house has been reoutfitted in its fresh summer garb, it is time to hang a windbell from the eaves and relax while listening to its delicate song. Fan in hand, lolling on cool tatami matting, appreciate how the Japanese approach to summer has created an aura of coolness for all five senses. Filtered light and cool colors, the fresh scent of reed mats, the dry touch of linen, the plaintive sound of the windbell with its promise of breezes, and the soothing taste of iced plum wine: summer can be tranquility and coolness, no matter what the thermometer says.

Water, splashed on a walkway and as a curtain motif, suggests coolness on a hot summer evening. The doorway curtain (instructions on p. 64) is made of a loosely woven, crisp fabric for summer. A basket lantern (p. 65) welcomes guests with its soft light.

DOORWAY CURTAIN

color photograph on p. 63

MATERIALS

linen or cotton cloth:
2 pieces, each 15″ × 45″

bamboo or wooden dowel:
½″ dia. × 30″–32″ long

NOTE: The doorway curtain presented here is decorated with the coauthor Kunio Ekiguchi's family crest and a flowing water design dyed using the traditional technique of *tsutsugaki* (cone-applied paste resist). You may use any surface decoration method you like—such as embroidery, patchwork, or tie-dye. Width of finished curtain is 28″ (30″ if Japanese yardage is used.)

1. Lay the two pieces of linen together lengthwise to form one large sheet. Sketch in a design and dye, keeping in mind there will be a seam allowance of ½″ along long edges and bottom of each piece (2¼″ along top).

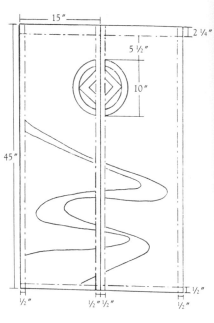

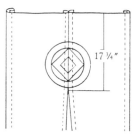

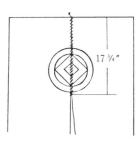

2. Sew together top 17¾″ of center seam, leaving a ½″ seam allowance and stopping at bottom of family crest. Turn under remaining center edges and both side edges, and stitch down. (If narrow Japanese fabric is used, handstitch top 17¾″ together, leaving no seam allowance, and leave other edges as is; the selvedges make hemming unnecessary.)

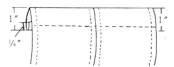

3. Make a casing for bamboo along top edge of curtain.

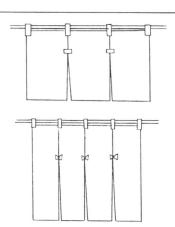

Doorway curtains (*noren*) can be made in a variety of styles. Length may vary from 1 to 5 feet, and the construction may include any number of cloth panels and loops for hanging. Just be sure the curtain overlaps the sides of the door frame. Loosely woven or somewhat see-through fabrics are most commonly used in summer since they suggest a light airiness.

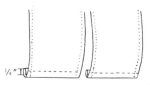

4. Turn under bottom edges in a narrow hem.

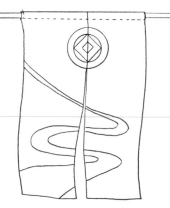

5. Thread dowel through casing and hang curtain on L-shaped hooks over a doorway.

BASKET LANTERN

color photograph on p. 63

MATERIALS

bamboo basket: 12 ½″ dia. × 21″ tall

translucent white paper (washi recommended):
6 sheets, each 7 ⅛″ × 19″
1 hexagon, 12″ dia.

electric light fixture: porcelain lamp socket with covered terminals, wire, and plug

wood:
1 board, same diameter as basket × ¼″ thick
2 pieces, each ½″ × 1″ × 6″

NOTE: This lantern was inspired by the custom of setting out candlelit lanterns at night to guide guests along the path from gate to doorway. The basket used here was designed to hold a fighting cock, but any open-weave basket can be substituted to make a charming lantern. Just cut off the handle (if present) and turn upside down.

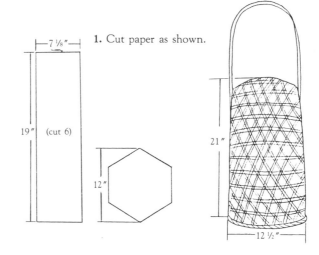

1. Cut paper as shown.

2. Spread glue over entire interior of basket. Let dry, then apply glue again.

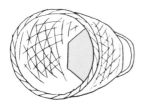

3. Glue hexagonal sheet to inside top of basket.

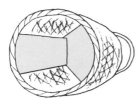

4. Glue in rectangular sheets so that they overlap hexagon and each other by about ½″ and completely cover inside of basket.

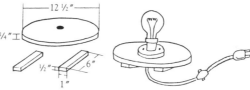

5. Spray inside paper surface with water to dampen, then let dry completely to make paper taut. Drill ½″ diameter hole in center of wooden circle. Glue and nail short pieces of wood to bottom of circle as feet. Send wire from lamp socket through hole, secure base of socket to wooden circle with screws, and attach plug to end of wire.

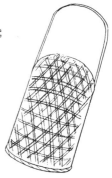

6. Turn on light (40 watt bulb is sufficient) and set basket snugly over base. (A more convenient alternative, pictured, is to use a cord switch—a switch several feet from fixture—so light can be switched on and off without removing basket.)

Windbells are made of iron, pottery, shell, or, as shown here, glass (instructions on p. 70). When the paper strip attached to the clapper catches the breeze and rings the chime's delicately beautiful note, summer's heat is forgotten.

The Japanese used to cool off in the evening by sitting outside on bamboo benches, taking in the summer scent of herbal mosquito coils and eating shaved ice topped with flavored syrup. Popular aids to keeping cool nowadays are thin floor cushions covered with summery fabrics (instructions on p. 68) and paper fans, whether decorated with subtle color (p. 69) or with a leaf (p. 132).

FLOOR CUSHION

color photograph on p. 66

MATERIALS

cotton fabric: 2 pieces, each 12″ × 24″

cotton batting: 5 sheets, each 23″ × 23″

embroidery floss or buttonhole thread

NOTE: To produce a more dramatic effect, use contrasting fabrics for the two rectangles. This pattern can be used with a single square piece of cloth, such as a scarf or *furoshiki*, to make a square cushion of any size. For ease of cleaning, you might wish to make an inner case of muslin or other cheap fabric, and sew in a zipper or Velcro instead of slipstitching last seam closed.

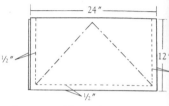

1. Place the two pieces of cloth with right sides together. Stitch a ½″ seam around three sides, as shown.

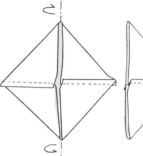

2. Open the unsewn edge, pulling outward from the midpoints of the edges and folding along lines indicated in step 1.

3. Open unsewn edge as far as possible, making cloth into a diamond shape. Fold in half into a triangle along unsewn seam, with the unsewn edges outside.

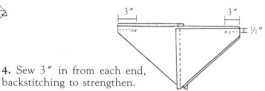

4. Sew 3″ in from each end, backstitching to strengthen.

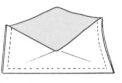

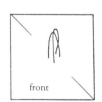

5. Turn right-side out and fill with layers of cotton batting. Slipstitch opening closed.

6. With the embroidery floss, loosely sew through all layers of cushion to make a cross on front; start sewing from back of cushion, leaving a 9″ tail of thread (with end unknotted).

7. From the back, pull up thread tail, the loop made in sewing the cross, and the needle end, as shown, so that each is about 9″ long.

8. Knot strands together in a simple half-hitch about 4″ above cushion. Cut off ends about 3″ beyond knot.

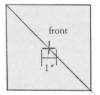

9. On right side, pull up strands and tie together firmly at fabric surface, dimpling surface of cushion slightly. Cut off ends 3″ from knot.

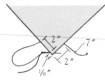

10. To make corner tassel, push needle into stuffing 2″ from corner on right side, leaving a 7″ tail. Pull needle out 2″ from corner on left side, then sew through corner, left to right, ⅛″ from tip, leaving a loop of about 11″ of thread.

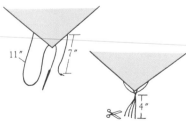

11. Pull up loop and strands and knot together at corner, cutting off ends 4″ from knot. Repeat for all corners.

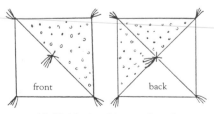

12. Finished cushion made with contrasting fabrics.

FANS

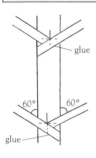

color photograph on p. 66

FAN WITH COLOR GRADATION

MATERIALS

balsa wood:
1 stick, $1/16'' \times 1/2'' \times 15''$
8 sticks, each $1/32'' \times 1/4'' \times 6\ 1/2''$

white paper:
2 sheets, each $8'' \times 11''$
1 strip, $2'' \times 24''$

NOTE: Japanese paper (*washi*) is recommended for all paper used in these fans, at it is strong and flexible. Balsa wood is substituted here for the split bamboo normally used in Japanese fans.

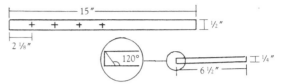

1. Mark the 15″ stick along middle at four 2 1/8″ intervals from one end. Trim one end of each 6 1/2″ stick, as shown.

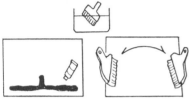

2. Arrange the eight 6 1/2″ sticks on one side of 15″ stick at the marks, and glue in place to make fan's frame.

3. Place both sheets of paper over frame of fan as shown and cut in a rounded shape, trimming off ends of frame ribs where necessary.

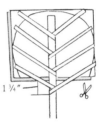

4. Moisten plywood board, then wipe off excess water. Apply poster paint to board in an upside-down T shape as shown. Dip one end of a broad, short-bristled brush in water, hold so water drains to one end of brush, then spread out paint on board with back-and-forth strokes, keeping brush at same horizontal position.

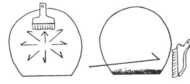

5. Lightly dampen one sheet of white paper with an atomizer, place on clean flat working surface (plywood, linoleum, etc.), and press out all air pockets with another (dry) broad, short-bristled brush, brushing from center to sides. With the paint-loaded brush from step 4, apply color with no more than a few horizontal strokes to the paper, lining up bottom of brush with bottom edge of paper. Repeat with second sheet.

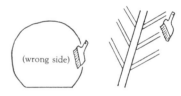

6. While painted sheets of paper are still slightly damp, apply glue to backs of both sheets and then to both sides of ribs and spine of fan, avoiding handle.

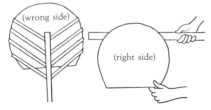

7. Press fan frame onto glued side of one sheet of paper, then lift second sheet with edge of flat stick or ruler as shown and glue in place, lining up bottom edges and carefully smoothing out wrinkles and bubbles with a dry brush.

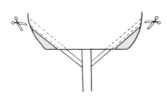

8. Let dry for about half a day and iron flat between scrap sheets of plain white paper. Trim paper edges to form smooth line, removing extra bits at bottom corners.

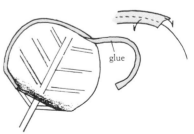

9. Glue paper strip around curved edge of fan.

Instructions for Fan with Leaf begin on p. 132.

WINDBELL WITH FERN

color photograph on p. 67

MATERIALS

bell:
glass bottle with secure press-in plastic lid, 2 ½″ dia. at base
glass tube, ¼″ dia. × 3″ — strong string, 13″ long
2 plastic straws, each ⅛″ dia. × 1″ — paper, 2″ × 8″

fern basket:
peat moss — fine wire
lump of humus — fine copper wire
hemp twine — thick copper wire, 14″ long
haresfoot fern roots (*Davallia mariessii*)

NOTE: These instructions are for making a ball-shaped planter, but feel free to fashion planters in other shapes—ships, wreaths, and moon crescents are among those seen in Japan. For best results, hang the windbell in the shade and water the fern frequently (two or three times a day). If haresfoot fern (*shinobu* in Japanese) or a similar fern with sturdy roots is not available, substitute a plant such as ivy. Whatever the plant, use roots gathered in early spring before leaf buds appear (around March in Japan).

1. File around bottle at the middle, where you want to cut it, deep enough so a string tied around it won't slip.

2. Tie a string soaked in kerosene around filed groove and light it.

3. When string is lit and burning around entire circumference, plunge bottle into cold water, holding it by the neck. The sudden temperature change will cause it to break neatly at the string. A glass saw, if available, could be used instead to cut bottle. Carefully smooth sharp edges with a file. (The "Edo windbell" is known for its gentler tinkling, the result of its jagged glass edge. You may wish to leave the broken glass edge unfiled; just be sure the bell is placed out of reach of children.)

4. Make a hole in the press-in lid.

5. Tie a knot around 1″ piece of plastic straw 5″ from one end of string. Then tie the straw in a simple knot. Thread other end of string through glass tube.

6. Tie another 1″ plastic straw to string, below the glass tube and 5″ below the first straw.

7. Pass the 5″ end of string up through bottle's neck and then through hole in press-in lid. Make a loop in string end and press lid firmly in bottleneck.

8. Make a hole in center top of piece of paper and tie other (bottom) end of string to it.

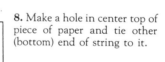

9. Form humus into a ball and wrap in peat moss to about 6″ in diameter.

10. With fine wire, wrap peat-moss-covered ball, shaping the ball neatly as you wrap, to make a pot-less hanging planter.

11. Plant the hanging planter by wrapping haresfoot fern roots in a spiral around the peat moss. Secure roots to peat moss by wrapping again with fine copper wire. Twist ends of wire together at the top.

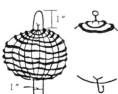

12. Bend the thick copper wire into a horseshoe shape. Thrust ends through hanging basket from top about 1″ apart. Twist them together at bottom, then curve up into a hook. Twist loop at top into a ring.

13. Tie hemp twine to ring at top of hanging planter. Hang glass bell by its top loop on hook at bottom of planter. Suspend assembled windbell by the twine from a tree branch or under the eaves where it will catch the breeze.

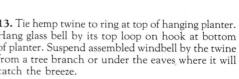

AUTUMN

early August
through
early November

The most dramatic event of autumn is the coming of the first typhoon. Born near the equator, typhoons reach Japan from August through September. With weather satellites on guard, a typhoon no longer catches anyone by surprise; there it is, a tidy spiral, right in the evening paper. But before satellite photographs it was still possible to sense a typhoon drawing near. The drop in the barometric pressure can be felt when the storm is six hundred miles away. The heat becomes intolerable, and, right before the storm hits, often the sky is metallic yellow over land filled with a tense stillness.

A typhoon brings strong winds and driving rain, with serious potential for damage to crops, roads, and buildings. If preparations have been made in time and the storm stays offshore, the howling winds and creaking buildings do not spell disaster. On the contrary, a typhoon in the vicinity helps refill the water reservoirs that typically dwindle by summer's end. And those who sit out the storm are lavishly rewarded with the brilliant blue skies and clean air that follow a typhoon.

In autumn, the *kinmokusei*, or fragrant olive, blooms. This common garden tree is grown for the intoxicating sweet scent of its tiny golden flowers, so well hidden beneath the thick foliage that only their fragrance or a heavy rainfall dashing them to the ground reveals their presence.

The scent of *kinmokusei* is likely to be accompanied by a harbinger of deepening fall weather, the red dragonfly. This insect comes down from the highlands in late September. The sight of a red dragonfly on a balmy September day is a reminder that the chill in the mountains will soon reach the lowlands.

If it is growing cold in the mountains, it is almost foliage season. Since Japan is so mountainous, fall leaves can be admired from late September through November almost anywhere if one is willing to climb high enough. The sight is certainly worth the climb; the mountainsides in fall are likened to brilliant brocades for good reason. The earliest trees to turn when the nightly temperatures begin to fall below 8°C (46°F) are among the most colorful. Japanese lacquer trees, sumacs, and maples flame into crimson. Famous sites—Nikko, Takao, and Hakone in the Tokyo area—bustle with good-natured crowds of appreciative foliage hunters, out enjoying the fall weather and the annual transformation of the mountains from green to red and gold. At home as well, the ornamental maple in the garden is resplendent, but the real star is the gingko tree, which, when its fan-shaped leaves turn a blinding yellow, becomes a beacon against the autumn sky.

Lunar double nine, the ninth day of the ninth lunar month, was the occasion of *choyo no sekku*, or the Chrysanthemum Festival. This day was, with the Peach Festival (the Doll Festival) on lunar double three and the Sweet-Flag Festival (Boys' Day) on double five, one of the festivals of Chinese origin marking a major change in season. Though it is now less commonly celebrated than the other festivals, the imperial court still observes it. In the Heian period, the court celebrated the Chrysanthemum Festival by composing verses on the theme of the chrysanthemum at a party attended by the emperor and by drinking chrysanthemum wine to avert illness and disaster.

A variation at the popular level is the Chrysanthemum Offering, now held on October 18 at the Asakusa Kannon Temple in Tokyo. Worshippers buy chrysanthemum plants, offer them at the temple, and then retrieve them on their way home. The chrysanthemums are thought to prevent illness and disaster.

Now late October and November are the time for serious chrysanthemum viewing. Public gardens sponsor chrysanthemum exhibitions with competitive entries in various classes of bloom—large, medium, or small, formal or ragged style, shaped as bonsai or not. The amazing variety of the entries and their warm fall colors draw thousands of viewers to the exhibitions.

In gardens and along country roads can be seen another dramatic display, that of the persimmon tree. An ordinary tree in spring and summer, the persimmon is transformed in fall. First the leaves turn red, then the fruit begins to turn a glowing red-orange. Powerfully sour at first, the fruit grows sweeter with each frost. When the leaves have fallen and the persimmons are sweet, it is time to harvest them, always leaving a few on the branches. The fruit are eaten fresh or dried. Persimmon drying is a community event—some peel the fruit, while others thread them on stout strings and hang them from the eaves in the autumn sunshine. The persimmons remaining on the tree are a treat for the birds that spend the winter in Japan, and a delight to the eye: each tree is a composition of startling beauty, a scattering of brilliant fruit amid gaunt black branches.

The bright red of autumn and the theme of maturation also make their appearance in a national holiday falling on September 15—Respect for the Aged Day (*keiro no hi*). On this day one gives gifts to one's elderly relatives, though it's not necessary to present the subdued clothing, reading glasses, and health aids promoted by the media as suitable. Local governments also honor their long-lived citizens. Such is the value placed on longevity that one town has decided to award one million yen to each of its citizens who makes it to one hundred years old.

This official praise for achieving old age is a public form of a much older custom, *choju no iwai*, or the celebration of longevity. Centuries ago the higher decades in life—from age forty on up—were marked with celebrations. With the diffusion of the Chinese calendar, the sixtieth birthday became the focal celebration, for in sixty years the cycle of the ten stems and twelve branches used to count the years has been completed. At sixty, one must return to the beginning of the cycle and thereby begin life as a baby again. Thus, sixty was the age to retire. To symbolize that setting down of responsibilities and return to the leisure of childhood, the sixty-year-old was given a bright red padded vest. Given the ingrained practice of wearing increasingly dull colors with increasing age, the substitution of bright red for the gray or dull brown suitable for an elderly person was a dramatic symbol of changed status.

Nowadays, given the diverse corporate retirement policies and desires of individuals, a family may privately celebrate the sixtieth birthday, but there is no accompanying change in social status. And turning sixty is no longer a remarkable achievement in a country that has one of the highest life expectancies in the world. Yet, the Japanese continue to offer respect, thanks, and gifts to the elderly on this day each fall in recognition of their contributions to family, community, and country.

The Seasons of Autumn

RISSHU 立秋

Risshu, or the Establishment of Autumn, arrives on August 7 or 8. While in theory the beginning of cooler weather, *risshu* actually brings the hottest days of the year, which are known as "leftover heat."

SHOSHO 処暑

August 23 or 24 is *shosho*, or Manageable Heat, one of the few apt seasonal names. September 1 or 2 marks a turning point in the weather. Considered an unlucky day, it often brings violent wind and rainstorms.

HAKURO 白露

In *hakuro*, or White Dew, on September 8 or 9, the weather is still quite hot, but the humidity starts dropping and the nights become cooler. Some birds begin migrating in this period.

SHUBUN 秋分

Shubun, the autumnal equinox, falls on September 23 or 24, right in the middle of Higan, a week of grave visits and Buddhist memorial services. The dramatic *higanbana*, a flame-red amaryllis, blooms along roadsides.

KANRO 寒露

Heavy dew, not quite turning to frost, is indeed characteristic of *kanro*, or Cold Dew, on October 8 or 9. The weather is mild and the air clear, lending a special radiance to the last of summer's lush vegetation.

SOKO 霜降

The First Frost, or *soko*, on October 23 or 24, is what it claims to be: in the Kanto district, the first frost does fall during this period. Leaves begin to change color and mandarin oranges appear in the markets—autumn has arrived.

The natural world virtually glows in autumn—warm earth tones dominate the landscape, foliage flames into color, pampas grass shimmers in the light of sun and moon. As typhoons give way to frost, the air grows clear and crisp, ripening the harvest and sending birds south.

duck (*kamo*)

chrysanthemum (*kiku*)

pampas grass (*susuki*)

maple (*kaede*)

persimmon (*kaki*)

The fine fall weather offers the perfect opportunity to gather chestnuts, gingko nuts, and edible mushrooms from the wild. Combine them with Japan's major crop of the season—rice—to create a classic autumn dish.

shimeji mushrooms (*shimeji*)

matsutake mushrooms (*matsutake*)

chestnuts (*kuri*)

rice plant (*ine*)

Rice mixed with seasonal delicacies: gingko nuts, shiitake mushrooms, and salmon (*top*) and chestnuts sprinkled with red *shiso* leaf flakes (*bottom*).

Flavors of Autumn

In Japanese, one usually speaks of eating a meal as "eating rice," and even today, despite the tremendous volume of noodles and bread that the Japanese now consume, rice is the leading staple. Just as in bread-based cuisines one distinguishes between breads that are tasty and mediocre, fresh and stale, white and whole wheat, so do the Japanese discriminate among rices. The strain of rice, where it was grown, how much it is polished, and above all how recently it was harvested—all make a difference in flavor. Gourmets eschew what is available at the local rice dealer's to order the best, freshest rice directly from farmers in a favored region.

Since new rice is available after the harvest in September and October, autumn is the season for savoring rice. Plain white rice is steamed rather than boiled. Electric rice-cookers have become nearly indispensable, but it is not difficult to cook rice without one. First the grains are rinsed, then combined with half again as much water and allowed to soak in a heavy saucepan for half an hour or so. Tightly covered, the rice is brought to a boil and simmered until almost all the water is absorbed. Next the heat is reduced to the lowest temperature possible for five minutes, and then the pan is removed from the heat and allowed to sit for at least five more minutes.

Basic white rice, delicious in fall, may be further enhanced by steaming other seasonal delicacies with it. The ultimate is rice with the delicious matsutake mushroom added. Since these large, aromatic mushrooms are not cultivated, you must either gather your own from the forests or pay a small fortune at the greengrocer's—one mushroom can cost more than a full meal at a good restaurant. Having secured a mushroom, slice it finely lengthwise to preserve its characteristic shape and marinate it in a mixture of soy sauce and saké. Add the marinade to stock, and use the liquid in place of water when cooking the rice. Just before the rice is removed from the heat, pop the mushroom slices on top. After they have steamed thoroughly, stir them gently into the rice and serve. The same method is followed when preparing rice using less precious mushrooms like fragrant shimeji mushrooms.

Chestnuts are another autumn favorite, eaten freshly roasted as a snack or, again, added to rice to make a classic fall dish. Chestnut rice begins with peeling, quartering, and roasting chestnuts. The roasted pieces are added to rice, the cooking water is seasoned to taste with saké, *mirin* (a sweet cooking saké), and salt, and the mixture is steamed as usual. Stir gently before serving. Sweet potatoes, harvested in fall, are another popular addition to rice. Make as for chestnut rice, substituting peeled, cubed sweet potatoes for the chestnuts and exercising great care when stirring at the end so as not to mash the potatoes.

The chrysanthemum, representative flower of autumn, also finds its way into rice. Yellow blossoms are most often used. The petals are plucked, lightly parboiled in vinegared water, plunged into cold water, and drained. A little sweetening is added to the rice, which is cooked as usual. The petals are added right before removing the rice from the heat, then lightly folded in before serving. The cheerful color of the petals and the contrast between their astringent taste and the slightly sweetened rice make chrysanthemum rice a light grace note among the more robust autumn fare.

Don't overlook the unlimited possible combinations of seasonal foods when steaming up a batch of rice—gingko nuts, carrots, and chestnuts with chicken bits, perhaps, or oysters, onions, and red peppers. Whether traditional or your own invention, such dishes will bring the essence of autumn to your table.

Moon Viewing

Twelve times a year the moon, companion of the night, is full. Its waxings and wanings do not pass unremarked, but only one of the twelve full moons is celebrated—the harvest moon of fall. In the lunar calendar formerly used in Japan, each month began with the new moon, and the full moon coincided with the fifteenth of the month. Thus, the harvest moon of mid-autumn would rise in the evening sky on the fifteenth of the eighth lunar month. That is the day for moon viewing. In the clear air of autumn, the moon rises huge and brilliant and makes its way majestically across the sky, as if to rival the sun in size and glory. In Japanese poetic conventions the "bright moon" (*meigetsu*) always refers to this, the full moon in mid-autumn.

Moon viewing, like cherry blossom viewing, intensifies the enjoyment of nature by making an occasion out of a natural event. The moon, however, does not require an expedition to be appreciated; it is always right out there, above the garden, visible from the verandah of a house or the balcony of an apartment. Also unlike cherry viewing, moon viewing includes offerings to the moon. A small table is set up facing east, the direction in which the moon will rise. On it are set out a pyramid of balls made of rice flour, perhaps melons or other round foods, taro, and an arrangement of *susuki* with other of the seven grasses of autumn.

The seven grasses of fall match the seven grasses of spring (which actually figure in New Year's customs). Unlike the spring grasses, however, the autumn set is not eaten but admired. Of them *susuki* is the only one that must be included in the moon-viewing display. *Susuki* is pampas grass, which grows wild on hillsides and unused land throughout Japan. Its tall waving stalks and graceful silvery seed heads are a potent symbol of fall—nothing is more lovely, or more desolate, than the sight of wind blowing across a patch of *susuki*. Use of *susuki* in the moon-viewing display implies a prayer for a good harvest with their allusion to Japan's premier member of the grass family, rice.

The other essential ingredient of moon-viewing offerings is taro, a tuber widely cultivated as a staple throughout Southeast Asia. It is thought that in prehistoric Japan, too, taro was a staple food before wet rice agriculture was introduced from the Asian mainland. The inclusion of taro among the offerings represented thanksgiving for the taro harvest, completed by moon-viewing time, and complemented the prayer for a good rice harvest.

Viewing the huge full moon of the lunar eighth month is paired with a second moon viewing on the thirteenth of the ninth lunar month. While the eighth month celebration was introduced from China, the next month's moon viewing is Japanese in origin and feeling. The date chosen is two days before the full moon. The preference for the beauty of imperfection, of incompleteness, a strong element in Japanese aesthetics, has dictated this choice of date. For this second viewing the offering table is again decorated with an arrangement of *susuki*, accompanied this time by *edamame* (boiled green soybeans) or chestnuts.

Which moon viewing to pick—the perfect splendor of the full moon in the eighth month or the more subtle promise of the nearly full moon in the ninth month? In fact, it is customary to view both. Among some groups, the highly superstitious courtesans of the city of Edo's gay quarters, for instance, to celebrate one and not the other was taboo. When the offerings are arranged and the moon rising, what does one do at a moon viewing? Gaze upon the moon, trace the patterns of its craters, and relax. Let its associations rise in your mind. Is the huge disk moving toward the west a reminder of the Western Paradise, a place of salvation to Buddhists? Does it recall fairy tales about

A gold fan, representing the full moon, sets off autumn flowers arranged in a bamboo vase (instructions on p. 81).

An arrangement of pampas grass and an offering of rice balls await the rising of the harvest moon. The rice balls are placed on a serving dish made of lacquered paper and rattan (instructions on p. 80).

the man in the moon or princesses dwelling there? Enjoy the nip of fall in the air, toss off a verse if you are so inclined, and gaze again.

The waxing and waning of the moon control the tides, a familiar phenomenon in Japan, with its long coastlines, and to the seafood-loving Japanese. Not only the tides but also women's menstrual cycles are in phase with the moon; in many cultures a leap in logic makes the moon overseer of newborn children, of love, and of arranging marriages. Again, the moon's monthly disappearance and rebirth leads to the belief that it controls the secret of eternal life. Thus, the Chinese moon, a relatively crowded place, is home not only to the god in charge of marriages but also to a rabbit who fabricates pills of immortality.

When, centuries ago, the Japanese adopted this story about the rabbit in the moon, they modified it: the Japanese rabbit in the moon spends his days pounding out rice cakes, a festival food but hardly one likely to confer immortality. That alteration seems to have been occasioned by the opportunity for a pun. The *mochitsuki* that means "pounding glutinous rice for rice cakes" also means "full moon."

The moon ranks with cherry blossoms in spring and snow in winter as the most important motif for its season. By the tenth century, the moon had become important enough of a theme to be included in the *Tale of Genji*; a man and woman meeting under the moon, moon viewing, and the moon reflected in water are discussed. This early novel also mentions another famous story with moon connections, *The Tale of the Bamboo Cutter*, the earliest surviving Japanese prose fiction. This story, based on folkloric sources, tells of a bamboo cutter who finds a baby in a bamboo stem and raises her as his own daughter. Called Kaguyahime, or the Shining Princess, she grows up to be as beautiful as her name promises and is courted by wealthy and powerful suitors, including the emperor, but she eludes them all by requiring them to perform impossible tasks. At last she explains to her earthly parents that she is from the palace on the moon and must return there. Sadly she departs for the moon, where even now Japanese children can discern her palace at moon-viewing time.

In art and literature, the autumn moon over a broad plain became a poetic fixture; the plain was Musashino, a marshy, wooded area now tamed by Tokyo's westward expansion. Its lonely beauty achieved its finest expression in the screen paintings of the Edo period, but one need not head for a museum to see the Musashino motif. Many Japanese re-create the motif each year at moon-viewing time with a few stems of pampas grass, artfully arranged, and the moon, real or symbolic, suspended above. Anything round, approached in the right frame of mind, can become the moon. A tray, a globular paper shade, a simple fan painted gold. A harvest moon over the pampas grass of Musashino, the same moon over a vase of the silvery fronds on a twelfth-floor balcony, or an ingenious representational arrangement indoors, far from the moon's beams—each offers the same opportunity to contemplate the season's natural beauty and rhythms and traditions, of which we all are a part.

LACQUER SERVING DISH

color photograph on p. 79

MATERIALS

paper tape (*kami teepu*) **or dressmaker's belt backing:**
19 strips, each ⅝″ × 8 ½″
4 strips, each ⅝″ × 10″

white paper:
1 strip, ¾″ × 48″
2 squares, each 10″ × 10″

rattan: 2 pieces, each ¼″ dia. × 27″
red lacquer (or nontoxic paint)

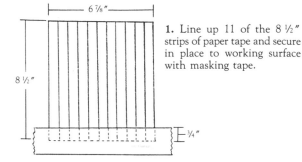

1. Line up 11 of the 8 ½″ strips of paper tape and secure in place to working surface with masking tape.

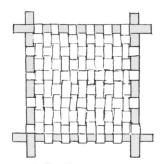

2. Weave remaining 8 ½″ strips of paper tape as shown.

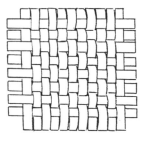

3. Results of weaving.

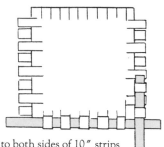

4. Apply glue to both sides of 10″ strips of paper tape and weave around edges of piece shown in step 3.

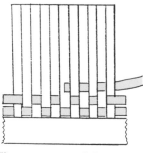

5. Finished weaving.

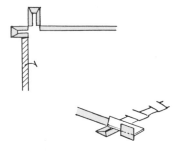

6. Fold white paper strip in half lengthwise and glue around edges of weaving, enclosing top and bottom surfaces.

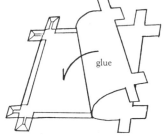

glue

7. Cut the squares of paper to size of woven piece and glue to top and bottom of weaving.

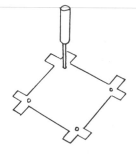

8. With awl, make holes in four corners of weaving slightly smaller than diameter of the rattan.

9. Bend up corners of woven piece.

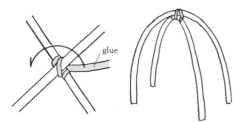

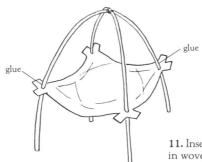

10. Tie rattan pieces into a cross at their middles with strong string and wrap joint with a glued ¼″ × 4″ scrap paper strip. When glue is dry, bend rattan carefully into arches as shown.

11. Insert four ends of rattan into holes in woven piece. Adjust length of legs. Paint all surfaces of serving dish with lacquer or nontoxic paint.

color photograph on p. 78 and front jacket

MOON FAN

MATERIALS

fan: 9″ × 15″

bamboo: ¾″ dia. × 7″

fine wire

gold and brown paint

decorative braided cord: 25″ long

L-shaped hook

assortment of autumn wildflowers

NOTE: Of Japan's seven traditional flowering grasses of autumn, five appear in the arrangement photographed—balloon flower, fringed pink, Japanese pampas grass, scabiosa, and boneset (*Eupatorium fortunei*).

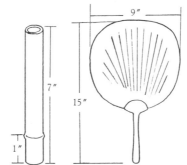

1. Cut the bamboo 1″ below a node (joint). Cut the other end so the entire length is 7″. Paint fan head gold. Paint fan handle and bamboo brown.

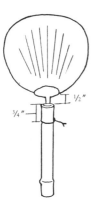

2. Attach fan securely to rear of bamboo vase with wire. If fan wobbles, you may glue bottom handle end to back of vase.

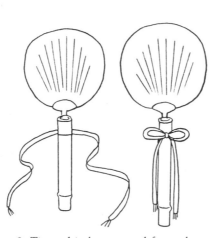

3. Tie cord in bow around fan and bamboo to conceal wire.

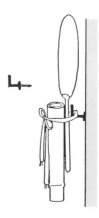

4. Secure L-hook to wall or pillar and hang up vase by slipping cord at back of vase over hook. Add water to vase and arrange flowers.

Warm up in autumn by sitting in a pool of sunlight and piecing fabric scraps together into practical expressions of the season. The traditional drawstring purses (instructions on p. 84) incorporate autumn motifs. Tiny scraps are all that is needed to make the thimbles (p. 84). The patchwork pincushion (p. 85) takes the form of a stylized chrysanthemum.

These colorful bean bags (instructions on p. 85) are filled with rice or dried beans, though a bell may be added to the stuffing for a cheerful sound.

DRAWSTRING PURSES

color photograph on p. 82

color photograph on p. 82

MATERIALS

FOR LARGE PURSE

fabric:
1 piece, 8 ¼″ × 25″
1 circle, 6 ¾″ dia.

lining fabric:
same as for fabric

cardboard:
1 circle, 6 ¼″ dia.

decorative cord:
2 pieces, each 30″ long

embroidery thread:
42″ long

FOR SMALL PURSE

fabric:
1 piece, 5″ × 13 ¾″
1 circle, 4 ¾″ dia.

lining fabric:
same as for fabric

cardboard:
1 circle, 4 ½″ dia.

decorative cord:
24″ long

embroidery thread:
18″ long

NOTE: Silk, used for both the outer fabric and lining in the projects photographed, makes an elegant purse, but any soft, flexible fabric may be substituted. These instructions apply to making either purse.

1. With right sides together, sew both outer cloth and lining into tubes. Turn only lining right-side out.

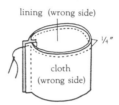

2. Place lining tube inside outer cloth tube with right sides together and seams aligned. Sew lining and cloth together around one end of tube.

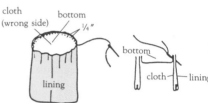

3. Turn inside out so wrong sides of lining and cloth are facing each other. To unsewn tube end, sew bottom circle of outer cloth, easing tube fabric to fit bottom circle.

4. Spread glue on one side of cardboard and center, glue-side down, on wrong side of lining circle. Fold protruding edges of lining over cardboard, gluing down.

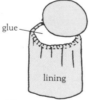

5. Fold over extending seam allowances at bottom of bag and glue to fabric on bottom. Spread glue on side of circle on which cardboard shows. Glue to bottom of pouch.

6. When glue is dry, turn pouch right-side out. Blanket-stitch very loosely around top edge with embroidery thread, spacing stitches 1 ½″ apart and ¼″ from edge. Start and knot off on inside of bag.

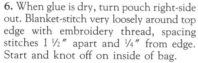

7. Starting at any point on purse edge, thread a cord through blanket-stitched loops, around entire edge, ending at starting point. Knot cord ends. (For large purse: Repeat with second cord, starting at opposite side of purse and threading cord along exact path as first.)

THIMBLES

color photograph on p. 82

color photograph on p. 82

LARGE THIMBLE

MATERIALS

fabric: ¾″ × 3″

lining fabric: 1″ × 3″

cardboard: ½″ × 2 ¼″

cotton batting: a small piece

NOTE: Wear either thimble on second joint of middle finger and use to push needle through fabric.

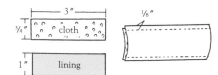

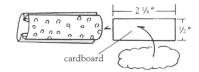

1. With right sides together, sew cloth and lining together at top and bottom, leaving a ⅛″ seam allowance.

2. Turn right-side out. Insert cardboard, centering in tube, and stuff cotton batting between cardboard and top fabric to plump out thimble.

3. Gather together cloth and lining at both ends and sew closed. Curve into ring with lining on inside and sew ends together.

Instructions for Small Thimble begin on p. 132.

PINCUSHION

color photograph on p. 82

MATERIALS

fabric: 8 isosceles right triangles (each with two 4″ sides)

lining fabric: same as for fabric   **cotton batting**

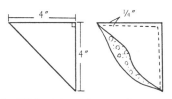

1. With right sides together, sew together eight pairs of fabric and lining along the two equal sides, leaving a ¼″ seam allowance.

2. Turn each triangle right-side out and stuff loosely with cotton batting. Baste closed.

3. Make a ball of cotton batting 3″ in diameter and ½″ thick. Mark its center top. Wrap a triangle around its edge placing far corners of triangle on center top and center bottom. Sew tips of triangle to each other, stitching right through cotton ball and pulling thread tightly.

4. Sew another triangle in the same way so that it overlaps the first. Repeat for all eight triangles. Tack triangles to each other at shoulder (see drawing) where tacks can't be seen.

BEAN BAGS

color photogtraph on p. 83

MATERIALS (makes 1)

fabric: 4 pieces, each 2″ × 4″   **dried beans (e.g., azuki):** approx. 1 oz.

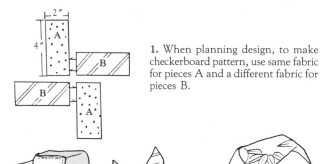

1. When planning design, to make checkerboard pattern, use same fabric for pieces A and a different fabric for pieces B.

2. Overlap one A and one B piece at right angles to each other, right sides together, and sew along three edges as shown, leaving a ¼″ seam allowance. Repeat with remaining A and B pieces.

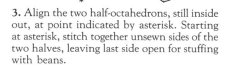

3. Align the two half-octahedrons, still inside out, at point indicated by asterisk. Starting at asterisk, stitch together unsewn sides of the two halves, leaving last side open for stuffing with beans.

4. Turn right-side out, fill loosely with beans, and hand-stitch closed.

Japan has a long tradition of making owls from *susuki*, or Japanese pampas grass, the fronds of which are wonderfully featherlike. The *susuki* owls sold in the fall at Kishibojin Shrine in Tokyo are particularly famous. (Instructions on p. 90.)

Autumn produces a colorful supply of natural materials that can be fashioned into everything from leaf dolls (instructions on p. 88) and traditional acorn balancing toys (p. 88) to rice-straw horses (p. 89) offered as thanksgiving for the completed harvest.

LEAF DOLLS

color photograph on p. 86

MATERIALS

FOR MAN

persimmon leaves: 2 big and (for sword) 1 small
pine needles: 2 pairs, each pair connected at top
acorn with bit of twig attached   **bamboo skewer**

FOR WOMAN

persimmon leaves: 6   **acorn**
pine needles: 1 pair (connected at top)   **bamboo skewer**

NOTE: Any similarly shaped colorful autumn leaves may be substituted for the persimmon leaves. If small leaves are selected, use a toothpick in place of the bamboo skewer.

MAN

1. For head, make a ¼″ deep hole in pointed end of acorn, slightly off center, with an awl or drill. Add dab of glue and insert bamboo skewer. Make sword by piercing small leaf with one pair of pine needles.

2. Fold large leaf in half. Fold second leaf in half and place on bottom, enclosing its tips within tips of first leaf.

3. With awl, pierce two holes through all leaf layers. Thread pair of pine needles through holes, starting at back.

4. Make hole at top fold of top leaf and insert bamboo stick with acorn head. Make another hole in both layers at left side, as shown, and insert sword.

WOMAN

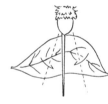

1. Make head as in step 1 for man doll. Wrap one leaf around shoulders as shown.

2. Wrap another leaf around shoulders, slightly lower than first.

3. Arrange remaining leaves in two stacks of two leaves each. Overlapping leaf tips, lay pairs over wrapped shoulder leaves. Make two holes with awl, piercing through all layers of both upper and lower sets of leaves. Thread pair of pine needles through holes, starting from back. Fold bottom corners of leaves to back.

BALANCING TOY

color photograph on p. 86

MATERIALS

acorns without caps: 3   **split bamboo:** 2 pieces, each ⅛″ dia. × 12″

NOTE: Piano wire may be substituted for the split bamboo.

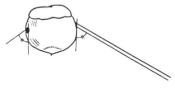

1. With pointed end of acorn facing down, drill two holes about same diameter as split bamboo pieces, one on each side of acorn. The holes should go in at same angle on both sides.

2. Drill a hole in top of each remaining acorn.

3. Insert split bamboo pieces into holes. Adjust lengths of bamboo pieces (by cutting) so that ends are at same height when center acorn is balanced on fingertip. Glue all joints.

STRAW HORSE

color photograph on p. 86

MATERIALS

rice (or other) straw: 50 straws, each about 30″ long

white cotton thread

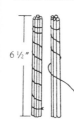

6 ½″

1. Cut enough 6 ½″ lengths of straw to make a bundle ⅛″ in diameter. Wrap with thread, tying thread ends securely. Make two such bundles.

1″

2. Tie the two straw bundles together 1″ from top with thread.

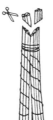

3. Make diagonal cuts at top, for horse's ears.

1″

4. For head, make straw bundle 1″ long and ⅛″ thick and wrap with thread. Slide down between ears so only one end sticks out; tie above head with string. This is horse's head and front legs.

3 ¼″

5. Make two bundles ⅛″ thick and 6 ½″ long. Join the top 3 ¼″ of the bundles together by wrapping with thread. Spray with water to dampen, then bend as shown.

6. Take several straws together and fold around front legs; tie with thread right behind neck. Cut to length shown. This is the body.

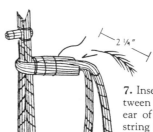

3″

3 ¼″

2 ¼″

7. Insert piece made in step 5 between body extensions. Insert an ear of rice for the tail and wrap string around all parts.

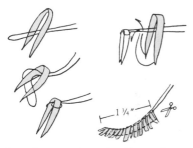

1 ¾″

8. To make mane, knot dried leaves from rice stalk onto a loop of thread as shown. Make mane 1 ¾″ long. Trim blades to uniform length.

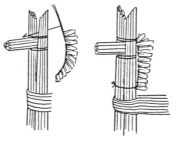

9. With thread ends on top, tie mane to head. With another thread, tie down bottom of mane.

PAMPAS-GRASS OWL

color photograph on p. 87

MATERIALS

pampas-grass stems with fronds: 30–40 stems

wood shavings or tiny red leaves: 2 (for ears)

twigs: ½″ long (for beak) and 1″ long   **black nuts:** 2 (for eyes)

NOTE: For the owl's features, use whatever bits of dried vegetation—stems, leaves, seeds, etc.—you can find outdoors.

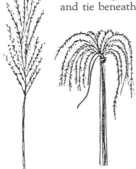

1. Stack together five pampas-grass stems and tie beneath fronds.

2. Fold fronds down around stems, plumping out to make head. Tie with string around neck.

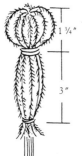

3. Tie down bottom ends neatly.

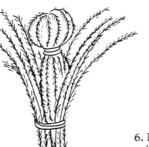

4. Arrange enough longer pampas grass stems around base to conceal it. Tie around stems over string tied in step 3.

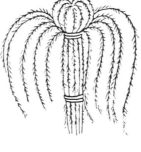

5. Tie the fronds tightly at neck and bend them down.

6. Plump out bent fronds, making extra fullness at left and right of breast, to represent wings, and demarcate wings and breast by leaving gaps between them. Tie bottom.

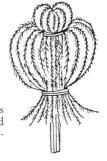

7. Cut out wood shavings and paint red (or substitute red leaves) and tuck in for ears, securing ends with dab of glue. Glue scrap strip of red paper around string tied at bottom. Glue on nuts for eyes and ½″ stem for beak. Cut off bottom of pampas grass evenly.

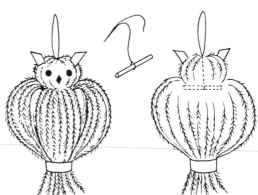

8. To display, tie one end of a red thread to middle of 1″ twig and carefully tuck twig under pampas grass at back of owl. Thread other end on needle, and stitch from back neck out through top of head. Remove needle, make loop in thread, and hang up owl.

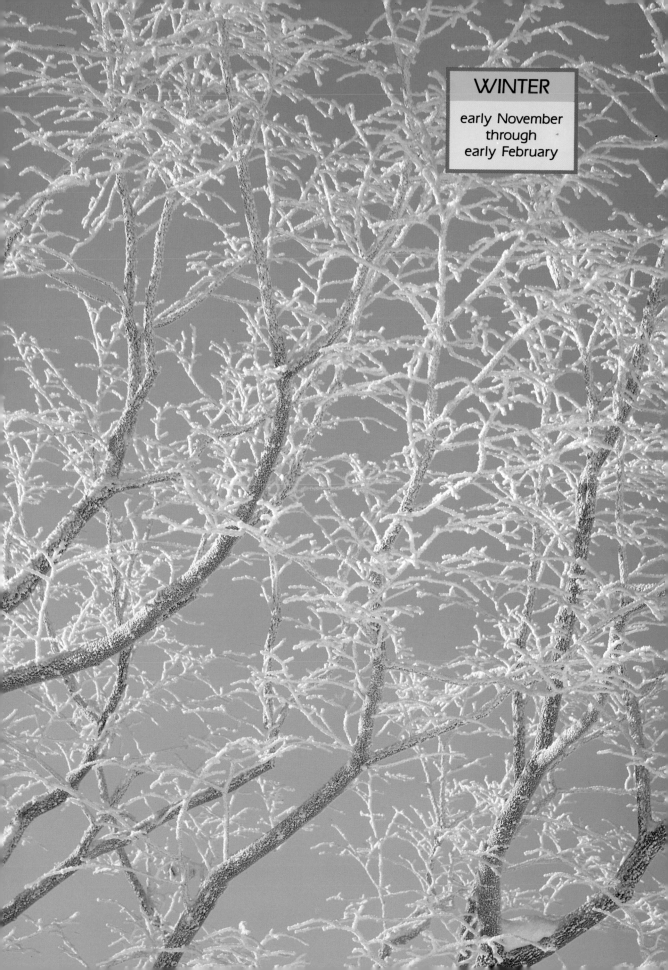

WINTER

early November
through
early February

Winter comes with a burst of color that rivals spring flowers and autumn leaves: children all dressed up in colorful finery on their way to the annual 3-5-7 ceremonies. On a brilliant November day, near the fifteenth, the celebrants—consisting of girls aged three or seven and boys aged three or five—are a splendid sight in every city and village. The girls may be in formal kimono, with brilliantly colored patterns and butterfly sleeves. The boys, in formal male kimono, display richly colored brocade *hakama*, or overskirts, a striking contrast to their plain underrobes. Both boys and girls may also wear equally formal Western clothes—velvet dresses for girls, suits for boys.

The children set off with their proud parents to a shrine. There they kneel before a Shinto priest, who performs a purification rite accompanied by offerings of thanks for each child's growth and prayers for his or her future well-being. Afterward, the children are given *chitose ame*, stick candy in long paper bags decorated with cranes and turtles, symbols of long life and good fortune. Then they are taken around to visit their relatives.

The ages of three, five, and seven have become customary for performing this rite, partly out of the Japanese preference for odd-numbered years, and partly because these ages were considered to mark major transitions in the life of a small child.

What does 3-5-7 mean today? For families, unquestionably, gratitude for their children's growth. For three- and five-year-olds, it brings unfamiliar clothing, fuss, and fun. But for the seven-year-old girls, it is something more—the first real occasion for dressing up. The glory of spending the morning at the beauty parlor, being coifed, made up, and dressed in a gorgeous kimono, whether rented, borrowed, or purchased, far outshines the shrine visit. At last the girl is part of the ladies' world of beauty!

In early December, after the last little beauty has returned from the shrine, it is time to think of end-of-the-year gift giving, called *oseibo*. As in the summer, presents are given to family members and to teachers, benefactors, and others to whom one feels obligated. Most gifts are food items, a reminder of the days when food was symbolically shared. Today, designer socks, antiques, and department store gift certificates offer other possibilities for giving.

December is also time to think about New Year's cards. Like Western Christmas cards, Japanese New Year's cards bear seasonal greetings and best wishes for the months to come. They differ in that all are delivered at once on New Year's morning. Many people take the time to design their own cards and print them with home printing sets. The cards are an outgrowth of the old custom of paying calls on New Year's Day. Some of the more important households would simply set out a box to receive calling cards instead of greeting their visitors, and in the late nineteenth century, with the development of efficient mail service, someone thought of mailing his cards instead of carrying them around in person. Now the poor mailmen are among the few who have to work on New Year's Day, delivering billions of cards across the nation.

The winter solstice on December 21 or 22 is the shortest day of the year and as such is marked by customs designed to ward off its dangers. A rice gruel with red beans is eaten to exorcise the plague god, who, according to one story, is afraid of this food. A medicinal bath is also advisable, particularly one that citron has been steeped in. Citron, which begins to ripen in November, is a citrus fruit resembling a lemon but with a distinctive flavor. It is thought to prevent colds and chapped skin, and soaking in the citrony hot water combines that salutary effect with a ritual ceremony of purification to strengthen the spirit as well as the body. You can also add citron's zest to soups and stews, squeeze its juice over grilled fish, or combine it with vinegar in a dipping sauce, and then toss the emptied peels in the bath for their fragrance, any day of the year.

Cranes are another winter sight. They arrive in Japan in October, winter there, then fly north in spring. These birds are notable for their pure white feathers, elegant forms, and graceful, dancelike motions. By the Heian period (794-1185), the crane had largely replaced the phoenix in bird-and-flower motifs borrowed from China. Widely seen in lacquerware, on mirrors, and in screen paintings, the crane is a beautiful symbol of long life and happiness. Learning to fold paper cranes is one of the first complex origami projects a Japanese child masters, and a chain of paper cranes embodies a potent prayer for life.

After the world has gone back to work and school, the New Year's celebration continues. On the seventh day of the year, for example, to prevent colds and other diseases, it is customary to eat rice gruel made with the seven herbs of spring. This custom dates back at least to Heian times, for Sei Shonagon's *Pillow Book* describes the court ladies searching on the sixth for tufts of green to pick for the next day's ritual gruel. When lunar New Year's was celebrated, and the search took place in our February or March, it was possible to find all the herbs: mugwort, shepherd's purse, cutweed, chickweed, bee nettle, turnip, and daikon radish greens. In early January, however, pickings are slim. While custom permits using only some of the herbs to symbolize the whole, modern marketing has provided a new solution: packages of all seven are available in supermarkets. Or, those who want the experience of picking the herbs can purchase a dish garden with all seven planted and identified.

The mild winter temperatures along Japan's coasts, from central Honshu south, bring narcissus into bloom in January. At the temple Zuisenji in Kamakura is Japan's best-known daffodil garden, which from mid-January through February is clothed in golden yellow. Not to be missed, however, are the natural narcissus gardens that established themselves where bulbs washed up ashore, possibly carried in on sea currents from the Philippines. The best examples of these tide-washed beds of wild narcissus are at Cape Echizen in Fukui Prefecture, where the bloom is at its peak from mid-January through early February, and at Tsumeki-zaki, Shimoda, on the Izu Peninsula, where the flowers nod between Christmas and New Year's.

The mild winters also give Japan winter-blooming camellias. Native to China, these bushes are covered with pink or red blossoms in early winter. Japan's native camellias, the *yabutsubaki* and the *yukitsubaki*, have been bred into more than a thousand cultivated varieties that enliven the winter throughout the country with their glossy green leaves and brilliant flowers. *Yabutsubaki* grow in thickets along the seashore and begin to bloom in November in warm regions or in early spring in colder areas. *Yukitsubaki* thrive in the deep snows of the Japan Sea coast, revealing their red blossoms after the snows melt.

The Seasons of Winter

RITTO 立冬

Ritto, or the Establishment of Winter, falls on November 7 or 8. The first chilly winds from Siberia reach Japan, stimulating the sasanqua (*Camellia sasanqua*) to bare its delicate blossoms.

SHOSETSU 小雪

The Lesser Snow, or *shosetsu*, arrives on November 23 or 24, but without the snow it proclaims. Apart from the mountain peaks and northernmost regions, Japan is still too warm for snow to fall.

TAISETSU 大雪

Taisetsu, or the Greater Snow, follows on December 7 or 8. It is a misnomer for most of Japan, as it brings only frosts and minimal snow. The yellowish flowers of *yatsude* (*Fatsia japonica*), a large evergreen bush, add an exotic touch to barren gardens.

TOJI 冬至

The winter solstice, or *toji*, falls on December 21 or 22. Adding fresh *yuzu* (citron) to the evening bath water and eating *kabocha* (pumpkin) on this day are said to guarantee one's health throughout the following year.

SHOKAN 小寒

January 5 or 6 brings *shokan*, or the Lesser Cold. Winds bear snow to the Japan Sea coast and mountains. *Shokan* is traditionally the time when winter training in martial and performing arts resumes after the New Year's holiday.

DAIKAN 大寒

Daikan, or the Greater Cold, falls on January 20 or 21. The last season in the solar cycle, it lives up to its name. At the same time, Greater Cold is the beginning of the narcissus season and of the annual renewal of all plant life.

Every winter climate has its natural beauties, made ever more poignant by the barren landscape and cold. The crane, symbol of long life and happiness, graces the snowy northern reaches of Japan, and winter flowers—such as narcissus and camellia—adorn more temperature regions.

crane (*tsuru*)

camellia (*tsubaki*)

adonis (*fukujuso*)

narcissus (*suisen*)

spearflower (*manryo*)

Nothing is so warming in winter as a one-pot stew, augmented perhaps by a flask of hot sake. Prepare the ingredients beforehand and gather around the table to cook as you eat, letting the rising steam, bubbling broth, sharing of food, and camaraderie work their warming magic.

saké (*sake*)

sukiyaki (*sukiyaki*)

yosenabe (stew of fish, shellfish, chicken, and vegetables)

oden (fish dumplings, tofu, and vegetables simmered in broth)

oyster stew (*kakinabe*)

Flavors of Winter

Japanese cuisine often emphasizes presentation over flavor, requiring attention to color, shape, and texture in the service of small amounts of many different foods. Each diner receives his own portion of the resulting collage of foods, and each portion is in its own dish. In the classic cuisine, serving informally from communal pots at the table is just not done.

Winter, however, brings relief from that rigorous approach. For winter is time for *nabemono*, one-pot meals cooked at the table over a charcoal, electric, natural gas, or propane heat source. With *nabemono*, everyone helps cook, tossing the prepared ingredients into a boiling, flavored broth and then fishing them out when they are done. The freedom possible with *nabemono* does not mean, of course, that ingredients are prepared for cooking any which way; a tray of sliced vegetables becomes a beautifully textured sculpture, a platter of beef a red rose. But once everything has been meticulously prepared, the meal becomes relaxed, with family members all gathered close together over the same steaming pot, eating at their own pace.

Sukiyaki is a *nabemono*, the most famous outside of Japan. It is a mixture of beef, vegetables, and tofu and is cooked at the table in a cast-iron pan. Other *nabemono* use a pottery pot to facilitate slow cooking; *oden*, for example, is a rich stew of daikon radish, devil's-tongue jelly (*konnyaku*), fish dumplings, potato, hard-boiled egg, and almost anything else appetizing, cooked slowly in a large ceramic pot and served, still simmering over a flame, at the table. *Yosenabe*, a hodge-podge of chicken, fish, shellfish, and vegetables in stock, is also cooked in a large ceramic pot, but its ingredients do not require long simmering; they are added, little by little, to the stock at the table and eaten as the liquid returns to the boil.

Shabushabu, another beef-based dish, is made in a deep copper vessel, filled with stock and brought to a boil at the table. The diners first drop vegetables in—Chinese cabbage, trefoil, shiitake mushrooms, and onion. Then, when the stock is again boiling, each person grips a paper-thin slice of beef with chopsticks, whishes it through the stock, and dips it in a mixture of sesame seed, vinegar, and soy sauce. The cooked vegetables are dipped in the same sauce and eaten, and finally noodles are added to the pot after everything else is gone to make a noodle soup rich with all the flavors of the foods enjoyed that evening.

Shabushabu is an extravagant version of *mizutaki*, a humble *nabemono* in which ingredients are boiled in plain stock. Another *nabemono* using the same technique, and perhaps the most elegant one-pot dish of all, is *yudofu*, or tofu in soup. The tofu is gently laid in the pot and covered with stock. Then the pot is slowly heated and simmered until the tofu cubes begin to float. Vegetables, such as fresh-tasting trefoil and rich shiitake mushrooms and green onions, are delicious additions. *Yudofu* can be eaten with a plain sauce of diluted soy sauce and sweetened saké or perhaps citron juice and vinegar, which bring out the delicious flavor of the tofu. As welcome as cold tofu in the summer, *yudofu* warms one to the very bone.

These one-pot meals are a timesaver for the busy holiday season. Any *nabemono* can be adapted to suit particular tastes or to use up what happens to be on hand. They are very flexible dishes, as they must be when the whole family is doing the cooking as well as the eating. Mere convenience is not the point, however. The warmth of *nabemono* is the special warmth of hot home-made soup. Sharing ingredients, offering choice tidbits to each other, everyone draws closer together in communion around the simmering pot.

Winter Warmth

Traditional Japanese houses are peculiarly unsuited to winter weather. They are uninsulated and drafty; all those lovely big sliding doors that are thrown open in summer leak heat horribly in winter. The tatami may also be laid over loosely fitted floorboards, under which there is nothing but cold air and frozen earth. The experience of trying to sit formally on the tatami in such a room while the draft from underneath rustles one's skirts is not one of the joys of winter.

Japanese families respond to the cold with sensible measures: exterior doors are weatherstripped, and all the *shoji* and other sliding doors that were removed for summer are replaced. Heavy, insulating curtains are hung. Carpets are laid over tatami. Beyond that, the basic strategy is to retreat into a smaller space that will be easier to heat.

In farmhouses, a square hearth is often set into the tatami in the middle of the main sitting room and filled with ash and charcoal. From a hook above hangs the tea kettle. With the kettle boiling, a pot simmering, or fish being smoked, the farmhouse hearth becomes the center of family life in winter, a place to gather, relax, and talk—there is no heat in the other rooms of the house. The fire must be watched, however, for the paper, straw, and wood of farmhouses is highly flammable.

A charcoal fire also glows in the *hibachi*, a deep brazier filled with ash, on top of which the coals are laid. *Hibachi*, made of brass, pottery, or copper-lined wood, offer more of a psychological than a physical warmth. A better heating strategy is the traditional *kotatsu*. When winter comes, a hole in the floor of the sitting room is uncovered. A small brazier with coals is placed in the bottom. A low table set over the hole is then covered with a thick quilt. Family members, wearing padded indoor jackets, sit on the tatami with their legs dangling down into the hole, the table quilt covering them up to the waist. The heat generated by the fire is trapped below the quilt, keeping the feet toasty warm while the head is chilly, a contrast regarded as the ideal stimulant for mental activity.

A *kotatsu*, unlike a *hibachi*, is actually quite warm. Moreover, family members are compelled to come together around the little table, to enjoy the warmth together. That combination is why, I believe, the *kotatsu* has survived while hearths and *hibachi* are rarities today. Apartment dwellers cannot have a proper sunken *kotatsu*, of course, but tables with a heating element built in under the table top are inexpensive and extremely popular, particularly with cats.

Eventually, however, everyone has to get up from the *kotatsu* and brave the cold. With careful planning, it is possible to go straight from *kotatsu* to hot bath. Then it is off to bed, where one can luxuriate under thick quilts thoughtfully and wonderfully prewarmed with a *yutanpo*, a flattish hot water bottle of porcelain, metal, or plastic placed at the foot of the bed.

Traditional approaches to heating in Japan are a primer for the conservation-minded: trap sunlight, close out drafts, and reduce the space to be heated to a minimum. The availability of electricity as a heat source has created a number of novel contraptions for fighting winter's chill. How about a pair of electric slippers, a desk with a built-in infrared heat lamp, or an electric rug? The electric rug is truly a brilliant invention; it puts the heat where it is needed and reduces the wasteful hot-ceiling-and-cold-floor effect. For a family oriented to on-the-floor living, and particularly one with small children, an electric rug is wonderful—if the adults can somehow train themselves not to keep falling asleep on it. And then, for a room often all too spartan and neglected, there is the electric toilet seat, a gift of winter's warmth indeed.

A folding screen (instructions on p. 100) blocks cold drafts, while a *hibachi*, or brazier, introduces heat to a room in winter.

The burning charcoal offers mostly psychological warmth, though the heat is sufficient to keep water boiling for making tea (instructions on p. 101) or for humidifying the dry air.

FOLDING SCREEN

color photograph on p. 98

MATERIALS

wood:

½″ × ½″   (A) 4 sticks, each 22 ¾″ long
            (B) 4 sticks, each 24 ½″ long
¼″ × ½″   (C) 10 sticks, each 24″ long
            (D) 2 sticks, each 21 ¾″ long

shoji-screen paper: 2 pieces, each 12 ¼″ × 22 ¼″

paper (washi recommended) or cloth tape:
1 strip, ¾″ × 24″

NOTE: Paper for Japanese paper screens, or *shoji*, comes in rolls approximately 12 ¼″ wide. If *shoji* paper is not readily available, substitute a 22 ½″ × 24 ½″ sheet of white paper. For a sturdier hinge, substitute metal hardware for the paper strip or cloth tape.

1. Cut tabs in both ends of each B piece, as shown.

2. Hold each B piece at right angle to end of A piece and carefully trace shape of tab. Cut slots in each A piece to match the tabs.

3. Apply glue to surfaces of joint and fit together A and B sticks, as shown, to make two frames.

4. Cut slots out of C and D pieces as shown.

5. Apply glue to joints and assemble C and D pieces as shown, to make two lattices.

6. Insert lattices into frames and glue in place. (Makes two screens.)

7. Generously coat one side of a screen with glue. Center roll of *shoji* paper vertically over bottom panel. Roll the paper on, as shown, covering the bottom panel first. (Working from the bottom up prevents creation of a tiny "shelf" at the papers' overlap where dust can accumulate.) Cut paper from roll with X-acto knife in straight line at edge so paper doesn't show on other (front) side. Use a straightedge when cutting for a neater line.

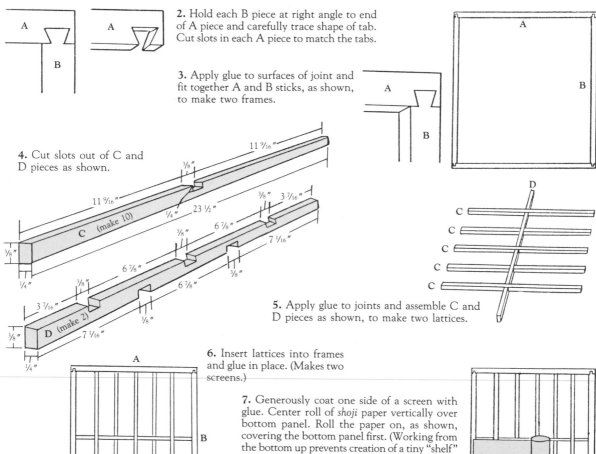

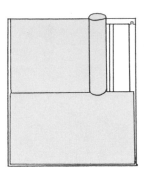

8. Cut off any protruding paper edges from bottom panel, then glue paper on top panel in same manner. Trim it also, then spray both paper panels with water, using an atomizer, while glue is still damp. Repeat steps 7–8 for other screen.

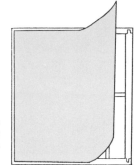

9. If roll *shoji* paper is not available, carefully glue on single sheet of paper without leaving wrinkles. Spray with water, as above.

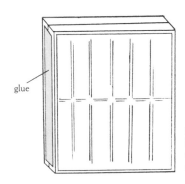

glue

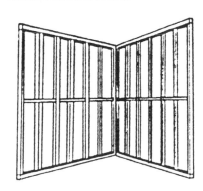

10. With paper-covered sides out, hold the two screens facing together. Firmly glue the strip of paper over joint between two B sticks. When glue is dry, open up and stand on A-stick side.

JAPANESE TEA

BASIC INSTRUCTIONS

1. Preheat teacups and teapot with hot water.
2. Boil water for tea.
3. Pour boiled water over tea leaves in teapot.
4. Steep for time specified and pour into empty cups, pouring a little into each cup and repeating until tea is gone. Strain as you pour if teapot doesn't have built-in strainer. Be sure to drain all liquid from teapot so leaves can be reused.
5. Serve alone or with decorative sweets or rice crackers.

NOTE: Making a good cup of Japanese tea is like making a good cup of coffee: there are as many ways as there are people. These are standard instructions for making the three major varieties of Japanese green tea, but do adjust them to suit your own tastes. Follow the directions for *bancha* to make its two popular variations—*hojicha*, a rich brew with a reputation as a health drink, and *genmaicha*, a popular beverage with a nutty flavor. All green tea leaves may be reused at least once.

MAKES 2 SERVINGS						
TEA CATEGORY	WATER QUANTITY	AMOUNT OF TEA	WATER TEMPERATURE*	STEEPING TIME	APPROPRIATE TEA CUP	COMMENTS
gyokuro	¼ cup	3 tsps.	(1) 40°C (100°F)	1½ min.	1 oz.	A delicate, fine tea for special occasions
			(2) 60°C (140°F)	½ min.		
sencha	1 cup	4 tsps.	(1) 80°C (175°F)	1 min.	3 oz.	A medium-grade richer tea to serve guests
			(2) hotter			
bancha	1½ cups	5 tsps.	boiling	a few seconds	5 oz.	An inexpensive, full-bodied everyday tea

(1) for first batch, (2) for second batch

Year-End Fairs

Fairs are closely tied to worship in Japan. Festivals at shrines are in large measure fairs, with hundreds of stalls selling food, games, and trinkets. Most fairs, in fact, are associated with some temple or shrine, even when they are not held on a festival day. It is likely that the earliest fairs in Japan grew up around regular religious observances, for any gathering of people encouraged trading, and occasions for trading were readily institutionalized as fairs. The religious significance of these fairs is also attested to by the participants' worship of a god of fairs, who has since fallen into obscurity, although markers inscribed with his name are still to be seen at old fair sites.

The end of the year is traditionally a good time for fairs; the crops were in, giving people the leisure to travel. The upcoming New Year's celebrations also required the laying in of supplies—ritual ropes and new soup bowls. Fairs before New Year's are still popular and offer an amazing range of goods: rope for tying the holiday ornaments, ferns, vegetables, seafood, miscellaneous hardware, footgear, dishes, toys, and almanacs.

The first of these year-end fairs is the *tori no ichi*, or "Rooster Fair," celebrated in November on the days of the rooster, as calculated with the twelve branches of the sexagenary system. Since each branch in a repeating cycle represents one day, November must have at least two days of the rooster, and the fair is held on both of them. Three days of the rooster in a single month augur disaster, especially fires, perhaps by association of flame with the red of the cockscomb.

Tori no ichi are held at Otori shrines, which are dedicated to the god of luck. The most popular fair site is Otori Shrine in Asakusa, Tokyo. The fair began largely as an agricultural implements market, but only one farm tool is now sold there, the *kumade*, or "bear's claw" bamboo rake. This tool

suggests the "raking in" of good fortune, an idea particularly appealing to the many merchants and restaurant operators among the Otori Shrine's devotees.

The *kumade* rakes are sold in giant to miniature sizes, and are so festooned with other symbols of good fortune that their original function is almost obscured. There may be a mask of Okame, a female good luck figure, or a rope to bind in good fortune, or a figure of the god of wealth, in addition to traditional auspicious designs, cranes for long life, and, bluntly enough, money chests. There is always room for one more lucky symbol.

The *toshi no ichi*, or "Year Fair," in December is the place to go for New Year's decorations and supplies. In the past these fairs drew people from considerable distances, come to stock up not only for New Year's but also for Obon in the summer. In the Tokyo area the oldest and biggest of these fairs is held at the Asakusa Kannon Shrine on December 17 and 18. There stalls offer just about everything, from buckets for drawing the first water of the year, to bonsai plants, lucky bows, offering stands, and decorations for gateways, alcoves, and altars.

Other big *toshi no ichi* in Tokyo are held at the Fukagawa Hachiman Shrine on December 14 and 15 and at the Kanda Myojin Shrine on December 20. Similar fairs are held throughout Japan. One of the oldest fairs in the Tokyo area is the *boro ichi*, or "Rag Fair," held in Setagaya Ward on the fifteenth and sixteenth of December and January. It began in 1574 under the protection of the Hojo lords of Odawara. With the decline of that family, the fair lost its importance, despite its site on one of the main highways of that time. But it never quite disappeared. Instead the *boro ichi* became a humbler market for farm tools and for the rags and used, tattered (*boro boro*) goods that have given it its name. Today the *boro ichi* no longer features many rags;

Rooster Fair (*tori no ichi*)

it is, however, an excellent source of potted plants.

Hagoita ichi are part of the *toshi no ichi* fairs and specialize in *hagoita*, the wooden paddles used in the New Year's game of *hanetsuki*, or shuttlecock and battledore. In Edo times these fairs were held from the sixteenth through the thirty-first of the twelfth lunar month. They now begin in Tokyo with the fair at the Fukugawa Fudo Shrine on December 15, and then go on to the Asakusa Kannon, Kanda Myojin, Yushima Tenjin, and other shrine fairs.

The battledores on sale at these fairs look like large ping-pong paddles but are actually ornaments, pure and simple. They are covered with figures of handsome actors and beauties built up in padded cloth to stand out in relief against the board. The effect is something like a three-dimensional ukiyo-e print. The original designs change each year to feature popular characters of the day or to refer to current events. A *hagoita* fair offers more imaginative design per square foot than many museums, as well as the good-natured bustle of the year-end crowd. A visit to the *hagoita* section on the grounds of the Asakusa Kannon, a part of the larger *toshi no ichi* there on December 17 and 18, makes a cheerful and colorful outing to work up some New Year's spirit.

A *kumade* rake

New Year's Preparations

New Year's observances are the most elaborate in Japan's ritual year, and they require no trivial amount of preparation, for at New Year's each household welcomes the ancestral spirits and the *toshigami*, the god of the incoming year. The preparations themselves must begin on an auspicious day. In most parts of Japan, *koto no hajime*, literally "the beginning of things," that is, the beginning of New Year's events, is December 13. On this day the *yang*, the masculine, positive principle, is at a peak.

New Year's preparations begin with cleansing to honor the *toshigami* by making the home free of all pollution. Families traditionally do a thorough housecleaning, casting out the year's accumulation of dust and cobwebs, throwing away useless odds and ends, and doing minor repairs. For instance, the old ripped paper is usually stripped from the *shoji* screens and replaced with fresh, new sheets free of holes (at least for the time being). While housework is almost always women's work in Japan, the *koto no hajime* housecleaning involves all able members of the family. Men used to stay home to do their share, but today, with less leeway in their work schedules, they generally cannot take an entire day off from their jobs. Instead, the family may confine the cleaning on the thirteenth to a symbolic dusting of the home altar, leaving the major housecleaning to a weekend, when everyone can be home to help.

After the house is clean, all the workers take a sip of ceremonial saké and then soak ritually in the bath to cleanse body and soul. Finally, after all their efforts, they can recuperate with some *okotojiru*, a soup of taro, daikon radish, carrot, and red beans.

In this way, all the pollution of the space and of the family's spirits is washed away. Cleaning the home on this scale and in this brief amount of time is a huge task. Everyone must participate, for if the job is not done well and if everyone's spirit is not purified, the household will not be fit to welcome the *toshigami*, who will watch over and protect it in the coming year.

December 13 is also a favored day for fulfilling all one's personal obligations, particularly in the Kyoto–Osaka area. Students of the tea ceremony and other arts pay calls on their teachers, bringing them *kagami mochi*, the large New Year's rice cake. Branch families similarly pay their respects to their main houses, as do independent branches of traditional businesses.

In some districts the thirteenth is also the day on which the *toshi-otoko*, the "year man," usually the head of the household, goes off to cut pine branches for the *kadomatsu*, the decorative display of pine branches and bamboo that will be set up at the gateway or entryway to the home. The *kadomatsu* can be as simple as a few pine branches and bamboo fixed to the sides of the front door, or as elaborate as the handsome, oversize sculptures in bamboo, pine, and rice-straw rope that are set out in front of department stores and corporate headquarters. The size of the *kadomatsu* is not important. What matters is that it is there; since the *kadomatsu* is where the *toshigami* manifests himself, it serves as the intermediary through which good health and prosperity for the coming year will flow.

To accompany the *kadomatsu*, families also stretch a rice-straw rope over the front door. Hung with folded paper strips, this rope defines the newly purified dwelling as a sacred space, ready to receive the *toshigami*. Twisting the rope out of rice straw was once the duty of the *toshi-otoko*. Today the ropes are bought at the fairs and stands that spring up at the end of the year to supply the ritual and practical needs of the holiday season. The rope, like the *kadomatsu*, is renewed every year and burned after the holiday. Similarly, a new *toshidana*, or altar for the *toshigami*, must be set up within the home.

New Year's requires *mochi*, glutinous rice cakes, all soft, white, and chewy. The time to make them is before the holiday, but not too much before, since *mochi* will eventually spoil. If families make their own *mochi*, in the seasonal event known as *mochitsuki*, they will do so from December 25 or 26 on. *Mochitsuki* was once a major event involving all the family members and their employees and relatives. Everyone would gather to take turns pounding away with a large wooden mallet at glutinous rice laid in the bottom of a mortar made from a tree stump. As one person wielded the mallet, another would flip over the mass of rice in the mortar after each blow and sprinkle it with cold water to keep it from sticking. The rhythmical thump-slap of *mochitsuki* is one of Japan's most distinctive seasonal sounds.

In urbanized Japan, most families do not own a proper mortar and mallet, much less have the space to use them. If they prepare their own *mochi* for New Year's, they probably use an electric rice pounder, a uniquely Japanese appliance that resembles nothing so much as the device the dentist uses for making silver amalgam for fillings. The outdoor, nonmechanized *mochitsuki* has not vanished, but has become a community rather than a family event. Neighborhood associations and kindergartens are particularly fond of sponsoring *mochi*-making festivals to give children a taste of tradition and most of all to allow everyone involved a taste of real, homemade rice cakes. These events do not, however, produce enough *mochi* to see all the families through the holidays, and most must fall back on using electric rice-pounders or ordering ready-made rice cakes from the neighborhood store.

The busy days right before New Year's are the time to close accounts, repay debts, and make sure that everyone in the family has the proper clothes for the holidays. This is also the time to make a New Year's Eve appointment at the beauty parlor to have one's hair put up in a more Japanese style (a must if one wishes to wear kimono) and to order in foods and ingredients for making *osechi ryori*, the traditional New Year's delicacies.

The last days of the year are a great rush of buying, especially since most stores are closed for at least the first three days of the year, and families and guests must all be fed during that time. The year-end is also the time to pack for train or plane trips, for New Year's, like Obon, is an occasion when families try to reassemble at the old homestead—and in so doing pack every train to many times normal capacity.

At last everything is clean, decorated, cooked, ready. It is New Year's Eve, and the country awaits the arrival of the *toshigami*. New Year's Eve in Japan is not for parties with silly hats and champagne, but for spending a quiet time with the family. Many families enjoy a late-night serving of *toshikoshi soba*, or "year-crossing" buckwheat noodles, to symbolize a wish for a life as long as a noodle. The custom seems to date from the Edo period and perhaps was only a clever marketing ploy by the noodle makers. But no one denies that a generous bowl of buckwheat noodles makes a delicious and simple meal to end the hectic New Year's preparations.

The final act to close the year begins an hour or so before midnight. This is *joya no kane*, the New Year's Eve bells. At all the Buddhist temples in Japan, monks and members of the congregation take turns striking the temple bells 108 times in succession. Japanese bells do not have clappers but are struck from the outside with a thick, horizontally suspended log. Each person in turn clasps his hands in respectful obeisance, pulls back the log with a rope, and then swings it forward to strike the bell.

The 108 strokes cast out the 108 evil passions that, according to Buddhist thought, beset mankind. Each temple is supposed to ring out the 108 sins every day, but most abbreviate the count to 18 except on New Year's Eve.

Bells as the final purification of the year seem perfectly fitting. Bells are eerie; they seem to have lives and voices of their own. In prehistoric Japan, bells were signs of authority; the bronze bells (*dotaku*) that have been discovered in archaeological digs could never have been rung but were purely symbolic objects. Bells are also among the objects that can be possessed by evil spirits—a popular theme presented in the Noh play *Dojoji* and in Kabuki plays derived from it. But the sound of bells also has the power to cast out evil. Thus, it was once the custom that a bell be struck before the emperor appeared, to protect his person.

Shattering the evils of the year one by one, the bells of Japan's temples toll out the old year, calming and purifying hearts too much caught up in the year-end rush. As believers line up to take their turn to strike the bell, a tally is kept on Buddhist rosary beads or with beans. One hundred seven strokes bring to a close all preparations; with the 108th, the New Year is here.

The New Year's Holiday

A *kadomatsu* decoration

The New Year's holiday in Japan is reminiscent of Christmas. Families decorate their houses with pine boughs, prepare traditional foods, give presents, and make every effort to reunite. The air is filled with the same excited bustle as the holiday nears—there are so many preparations to be made, and everything needs to be done with care. The timing is right, too, since both Christmas and New Year's come after the winter solstice, after the sun has begun to renew itself. A year without a celebration at this time would not be much of a year at all.

All the preparations before New Year's in Japan lead up to welcoming the *toshigami*, the god of the year, to spend the first three days of the new year with the family. During those three days, businesses and government offices are all closed; the world turns from the everyday and profane to the exalted and sacred. The word *toshi*, which now means "year," originally meant "rice." Thus, the god of the year is the god of rice—appropriately enough in a culture originally based on rice agriculture. The *toshigami* brings strength and good fortune, but if the preparations to greet him are not made properly, he will not come, and the year will not be renewed.

By New Year's Eve the house and its inhabitants are clean, physically and spiritually, and a rope has been hung above the entrance to denote the purity within and separate it from the pollution of the world outside. Decorative pine boughs, the *kadomatsu*, have been placed at the entrance to serve as a temporary resting site for the *toshigami* when he arrives. Inside, a new *toshigami* altar has been installed, trimmed with white, elaborately cut paper. Rice cakes have been made, the holiday food prepared, and all debts and obligations cleared up.

In the *tokonoma*, the decorative alcove in the best sitting room of the house, are a seasonal hanging scroll and flower arrangement. Displayed on the

Traditional New Year's foods

A straw rope marks a purified home.

Rice-ball display in the family altar

household altar is *kagami mochi*, two flattened balls of pounded, glutinous rice, the smaller placed atop the larger. The *kagami mochi* sits on pure white paper on an offering stand and is decorated with objects with auspicious connotations. These objects vary from family to family and district to district, but they are usually chosen for the lucky ideas suggested by puns on their names. The *kagami mochi* is often topped, for instance, by a bitter orange called a *daidai*, a pun on "generation after generation," and accompanied by persimmons ("joy") and lobster ("long life"). The same objects are also used in flower arrangements and other New Year's decorations—such as those tied to automobile grills and bicycle baskets, for example.

The preparation of the home as a sacred space to receive the *toshigami* is underscored in some families by the custom of making a shrine visit lasting from New Year's Eve to New Year's Day to bring home live coals from the sacred fire for use in preparing food during the holiday. On the morning of New Year's Day, the head of the household draws the first water of the new year from a well or spring that lies in an auspicious direction—a custom more often kept up in the countryside than in the city, where few wells and springs are available. The water is carried home in a brand-new bucket and ladled out with a new dipper as an offering to the altar for the *toshigami*. It is then used to make tea or the New Year's soup, *ozoni*. The household head also makes *otoso*, a sweetened saké in which medicinal herbs have been steeped. After the *otoso* has been offered to the *toshigami*, the whole family imbibes to ensure health throughout the year.

Otoso is served with a distinctive set of decorative implements. They consist of a lacquer stand, a teapot-like decanter, and three cups, large, medium, and small, displayed in a stack in ascending order of size. The decanter usually has an origami and wrapped-wire decoration attached to it between the handle and the spout. This ornament often takes the form of a pair of butterflies, male and female, suggesting marital harmony.

Recipes for *ozoni*, the New Year's soup, are highly regionalized. Most call for square, firm rice cakes in a plain broth with a few vegetables and fish, shrimp, roe, or other delicacies. In some areas, however, buckwheat or barley dumplings replace the rice cakes.

After the *ozoni*, everyone samples *osechi*, the traditional New Year's foods. *Osechi* is prepared in advance and handsomely arranged in layered boxes for serving throughout the first three days of the year. They are commonly assumed to be foods that keep well so that the women of the family can enjoy a respite from the daily cooking and ricemaking at the beginning of the year. But the primary role of *osechi* is as an offering to the *toshigami*. Thus all the New Year's foods have some symbolic or ritual meaning. The many foods packed into the *osechi* boxes, for example, must include small dried sardines, the characters for whose name means "working wet rice fields." Other foods may be chosen for their auspicious connotations—kelp rolls, say, the name being a pun on the word for happiness.

The first layer of a typical *osechi* box might include the dried sardines; kelp rolls; omelet slices; fish roe soaked in brine, then simmered; sweetened black beans; and pink-and-white slices of fish cake. The second layer could include grilled chicken, squid, shrimp, bonito, and yellowtail; hard-boiled eggs lightly chopped and reassembled into a log, then sliced; and pressed flaked chicken. After all that heavy protein, the third layer could include lighter foods: pickled fish; lotus root in vinegar; little vinegared shad roll-ups; pickled turnips cut to resemble chrysanthemums; cod roe in lemon cups; and pickled daikon radish and carrot strips.

In addition to picking foods that can be heavily sugared or pickled to keep without refrigeration over the three days of New Year's, the cook tries to make each layer in the *osechi* box a composition as colorful and joyful as the season itself. Color contrasts are used to define an overall pattern—a checkerboard or diagonal stripes, for instance. Each successive layer may be arranged in a different pattern to add to the visual interest.

New Year's morning has special significance for children: it is when their parents give them presents of money, or *otoshidama*. The amount varies with the age of the child and family circumstances, but it usually adds up to a substantial sum, enough, say, to buy a bicycle. Children are encouraged to bank most of their *otoshidama* earnings after spending part of them on toys, records, or treats for themselves.

The first day of the new year is usually a family day, spent quietly at home playing New Year's games or out making the first shrine visit, or *hatsumode*. In urban areas, people choose big, popular shrines and temples for the New Year's visit. The vast crowds—hundreds of thousands of people, all patiently waiting their turn to stand before the shrine and pray for a good year—are part of the

A lacquer set for serving *otoso*, the New Year's saké

experience. Everyone is usually very well dressed in new or at least fine clothing. An unusually large proportion of the crowd, men and women, are in kimono, for Japan's traditional dress is increasingly reserved for such sacred and festive occasions. Unmarried girls are an especially glorious sight in their gaily colored kimono, often topped with a little stole of fur to keep off the January chill.

At the end of New Year's Day, one goes to bed to dream. The first dream of the year will be a clue to the nature of the coming year, but there is no rule against trying to influence the outcome. The dreamer may, for instance, sleep on a picture of a *takara-bune*, the ship carrying the seven gods of good fortune, to ensure an auspicious dream.

The second and third days of the new year are for paying calls on friends and business acquaintances. Visitors give *otoshidama* to the children of the household, adding to their booty, and are served *otoso*. The fourth day of the year formally marks the start of work, including the year's first sewing, calligraphy, or hoeing. These first efforts of the year are symbolic; the actual work begins later. Office workers, for instance, do turn up for work on the fourth, but usually only to perform a formal toast. Some working women come to the office in formal kimono on this day.

Even New Year's has to end sometime. The date varies by locality, but the seventh day, when families eat rice gruel with the seven herbs of spring, is a common ending point. The New Year's decorations are then burned as a beacon fire to light the deities' way home, and the busy, profane world asserts its primacy again.

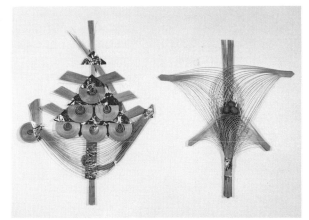

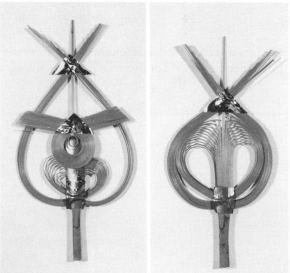

Bamboo decorations (*mikikuchi*) are inserted in the decanter when saké is offered to the god of the year.

Indoor New Year's decorations may include twining willow branches (instructions on p. 112), here studded with popcorn to represent plum blossoms. Gold and silver folding fans (p. 112) auspiciously suggest the future opening out. Radish rabbits (p. 113) should last longer indoors than their snow prototypes. A green bamboo vase (p. 113) is elegantly decorated with a white *noshi* and *mizuhiki* strings.

Displayed outside the home is the *kado-matsu*, or pine and bamboo decoration (instructions on p. 114). This version includes pine and bamboo, both good luck symbols, and a dangling white paper streamer as an offering to the god of the year.

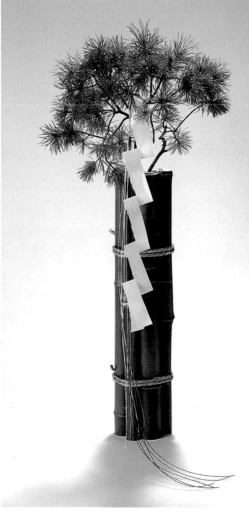

TWINING WILLOWS

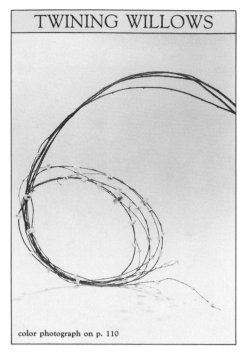

color photograph on p. 110

MATERIALS

willow branches: 2 or 3, each ¾″ dia. × 6–7 feet long

popcorn (popped): about 1 cup

1. Use slender, flexible willow branches cut before leaves or buds start sprouting.

2. Bind cut ends of branches together with adhesive or other tape. Coil branches into a circle, and wind tips around the circle. Branches should stay in place.

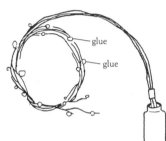

glue
glue

3. Glue popcorn "plum blossoms" to circle with glue. Insert cut ends of branches in a heavy flower vase.

FAN DECORATION

color photograph on p. 110

MATERIALS

folding fans:
1 silver fan, 7″ long
1 gold fan, 7″ long

single-strand mizuhiki:
1 strand of gold, 12″ long
1 strand of silver, 12″ long

sprig of blossoming plum

NOTE: Fans colored silver on one side and gold on the reverse side are readily available in Japan. To achieve the same effect, brush or spray gold and silver paint onto inexpensive paper folding fans.

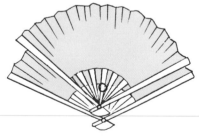

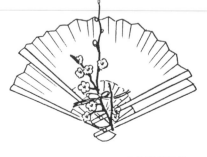

1. Open fans and place one on top of the other, offsetting slightly. With *mizuhiki* strands, tie fans together in a simple knot at the point indicated.

2. Place plum sprig over *mizuhiki* knot and tie in place with a decorative flat square knot. Cut off excess *mizuhiki*, leaving 2″ long ends. Hang fan decoration on door or wall, or use in centerpiece display.

SNOW RABBITS

color photograph on p. 110

NOTE: To prolong life of rabbits, spray lightly with water when radish surface begins to look dry. Rabbits should last five or six days at room temperature with no care.

MATERIALS (makes 2 rabbits)

daikon radish (or white radish): 1 piece, 2″ dia. × 1″

long narrow leaves: 4 leaves, each 2″ long

glass-headed pins: 4 red pins

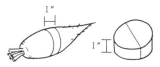

1. Cut 1″ slice from middle of daikon radish. Cut slice into two semicircles.

2. Make holes for ears with toothpick. Insert leaves in holes. Press in pins for eyes. Arrange on red tray and display.

BAMBOO VASE

color photograph on p. 111

MATERIALS

bamboo: 1 piece, 2″ dia. × approx. 11″

5-strand gold-and-silver mizuhiki: 40″ long

white paper: 2 sheets, each 10″ × 11 ½″

rice stalk with grains intact **camellia (or other seasonal flower)**

NOTE: Use freshly cut green bamboo. The variety used here is giant bamboo (*Phyllostachys pubescens*; *mosochiku* in Japanese).

1. Cut bamboo straight across 1″ below a node (joint). Cut other end diagonally to make a 9″ vase.

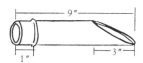

2. Stack sheets of white paper and fold in half twice. Then fold down topmost layer of paper as shown.

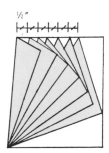

3. Fold down second layer of paper along line running from bottom left corner of square to point at top edge ½″ to left of first fold. Repeat for all remaining layers.

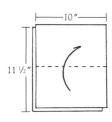

4. Tie folded paper to bamboo with *mizuhiki* in a flat square knot. Bend *mizuhiki* up into large circle, as shown, and twine ends around circle.

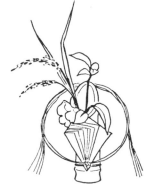

5. Fill bamboo vase with water and arrange rice stalk and camellia.

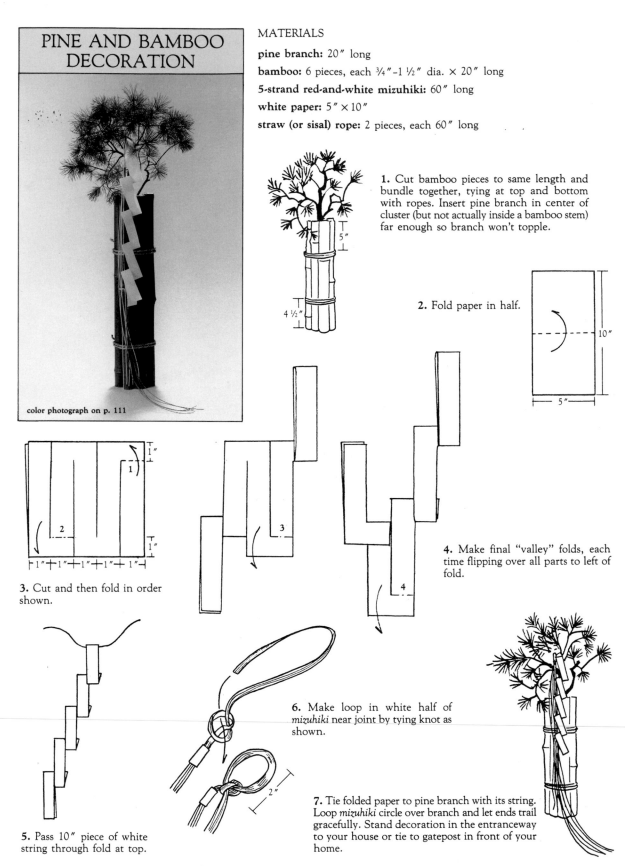

PINE AND BAMBOO DECORATION

MATERIALS

pine branch: 20″ long

bamboo: 6 pieces, each ¾″–1 ½″ dia. × 20″ long

5-strand red-and-white mizuhiki: 60″ long

white paper: 5″ × 10″

straw (or sisal) rope: 2 pieces, each 60″ long

color photograph on p. 111

5″

4 ½″

1. Cut bamboo pieces to same length and bundle together, tying at top and bottom with ropes. Insert pine branch in center of cluster (but not actually inside a bamboo stem) far enough so branch won't topple.

2. Fold paper in half.

10″

5″

1″

1

2

1″

├─1″─┼─1″─┼─1″─┼─1″─┼─1″─┤

3. Cut and then fold in order shown.

3

4

4. Make final "valley" folds, each time flipping over all parts to left of fold.

6. Make loop in white half of *mizuhiki* near joint by tying knot as shown.

2″

5. Pass 10″ piece of white string through fold at top.

7. Tie folded paper to pine branch with its string. Loop *mizuhiki* circle over branch and let ends trail gracefully. Stand decoration in the entranceway to your house or tie to gatepost in front of your home.

New Year's Games

The holiday days of New Year's are spent with the family together, relaxing and enjoying a respite from ordinary cares and enjoying some special New Year's games. *Hanetsuki*, or shuttlecock and battledore, is the girls' game. It originated as a New Year's event at the imperial court, a sort of polo in which mounted players with flat bats vied to see who could be the first to scoop a ball into the goal. In later centuries it became the custom to give these bats as New Year's presents. Gradually the bats shrank into the decorated battledores, or *hagoita*, of today, with which a single player tries to keep her shuttlecock aloft or two players hit it back and forth in a netless version of badminton.

The shuttlecock is now made of feathers and a soapberry seed, but earlier a bean was used in place of the seed. Beans have the ability to ward off plague gods and chase away demons in Japan. The girl whacking at her shuttlecock bean was, then, casting out evil and disease from the family, just as beans are thrown to cast out devils in the *setsubun* ceremony in February.

For boys, the prescribed New Year's game is kite flying. A light bamboo frame stretched with boldly painted paper can be a work of art in the hands of a Japanese kitemaker. Some kites have geometric motifs, while others are decorated with legendary warriors, characters from folklore, designs based on Chinese characters and the Japanese syllabaries, or animal figures. Making and flying these magnificent kites became a popular pastime in the Edo period. Kite battles were a favorite sport.

Kites were not simply playthings, however. They may have had an explicit religious function long ago, as the physical embodiment of prayers linking heaven and earth or as offerings to the gods. Even today kites are sent aloft at New Year's, and giant kites are burned to ensure prosperity and safety. Grandparents give their grandchildren kites at

Battledores

Hyakunin Isshu

Kites

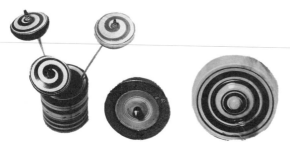

Toy tops

their first Girls' Day in March or Boys' Day in May, and kite flying is associated with Obon as well. Thus, boys struggling with their kites in the cutting winds of January are not only keeping New Year's sacred through play but also offering up a prayer—quite apart from their prayer that their kite strings will hold up.

New Year's recreations also include lighthearted games such as *hobiki*, a sort of grab bag in which a player picks one of several strings to pull. The strings are attached to labels hidden behind a screen, and the object is to guess which string leads to the best prize. Then there is *sugoroku*, a board game something like Parcheesi. *Fuku warai*, or the funny-face game, is a favorite, one that everyone in the family can enjoy. Using the outline of a face, with eyebrows, eyes, nose, and mouth cut out separately, the player, blindfolded, tries to put all the parts together. The preposterous results are an occasion for much merriment.

Hyakunin Isshu, however, is the premier New Year's game. As its name, meaning "a single poem by each of a hundred poets," suggests, it is a literary game. Winning depends on how well a player has memorized the poems. The *Hyakunin Isshu* poems were selected in the early thirteenth century by Fujiwara no Teika, the illustrious court poet who was one of the compilers of the *Shinkokinshu*, one of the greatest of the imperial poetry anthologies. Teika intended the hundred poems as a primer for his students; as such, they have been memorized by most literate Japanese for the past seven hundred years.

Teika's selection of exemplary poems became a New Year's game, also known as *uta karuta*, or poem cards, by a rather circuitous route. Playing cards were introduced into Japan by the Portuguese in the sixteenth century; *karuta* is clearly a borrowed word. At first the Japanese made faithful copies of the decks of cards the Portuguese played with. The cards and card games were sophisticated new entertainments, and spread rapidly among the more privileged samurai classes before becoming popular among the common people in the Edo period.

There also existed a game that had been popular in the Heian period and that was still being played among the court nobility—*kaiawase*, or shell matching. The game requires 180 pairs of large clam shells, dealt face down. The object is to collect as many matching shell pairs as possible. Originally the shells were undecorated inside; a match was determined by whether the top and bottom shells fit at the hinge. Then people began painting the temptingly smooth, white interiors with scenes from the *Tale of Genji* and other literary works. Matching shells were decorated with the same scene.

In the seventeenth century, someone among the noble families in Kyoto had an exciting idea: instead of cumbersome, expensive shells, why not use those new paper cards for the game? And why not go beyond the literary scenes depicted on the shells to make everybody's poetic primer, Teika's *Hyakunin Isshu*, part of the game? An order went out for pasteboard rectangles in pairs, one bearing the start of a poem, the other its ending, and *uta karuta* was born.

At first the game was a simple scramble, with all players silently trying to assemble the pairs of cards to complete the poems. By 1700 or so, however, the game had achieved its present form; the begin-

ning cards are shuffled, the ending cards are spread out face up on the tatami, and one player intones the beginning of a poem, while the rest race to spot the card that will complete it.

The game soon become so popular that by 1700 or so the cards were printed with woodblocks instead of by hand to meet the demand. By this time the game, which originally had no seasonal associations, had developed a fixed connection with New Year's.

Now a sure sign that the year-end is approaching is the appearance of *Hyakunin Isshu* sets, tapes of the poems, and explications of their meanings in the bookstores. New Year's is coming, goes the message, and this year surely you will want to become better acquainted with your poetic heritage and cut a better figure in the family game.

Hanafuda, a card game especially popular around New Year's

New Year's games range from flying kites—like this square kite (instructions on p. 120) and warrior kite (p. 133)—to spinning tops (p. 120). The best-known New Year's game is battledore and shuttlecock (p. 121), a traditional girls' game resembling badminton.

The funny-face game (instructions on p. 121) is for the whole family. A blindfolded player assembles cutout features on the board to form what he or she hopes is a face. The comic results generate much merriment.

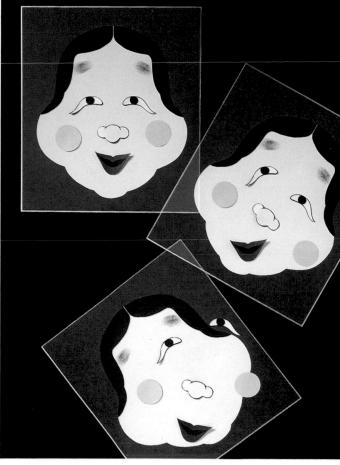

KITES

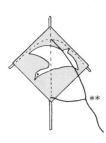

color photograph on p. 118

SQUARE KITE

MATERIALS

split bamboo:
1 piece, 1/16″ dia. × 17″
1 piece, 1/16″ dia. × 19″

kite string

white paper:
1 sheet, 11″ × 11″
1 strip, 1″ × 30″–40″

strong cotton thread

NOTE: Asterisks indicate the type of knot required. (See diagram to left for instructions.) Generally, * knots are for thread, ** knots are for kite string.

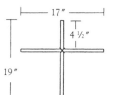

1. Arrange split bamboo pieces in a cross, glue joint, then tie securely with thread.

2. Curve shorter bamboo piece to tip-to-tip length of 14″ and tie thread to ends, like bowstring, to hold in place. Tie another thread around four ends of bamboo pieces to make square of thread.

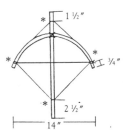

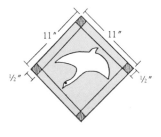

3. Paint a picture on square of paper, leaving a 1/2″ margin around edges. Cut out and discard corner pieces.

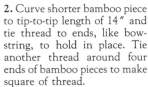

glue

glue

4. Spread glue on reverse side of 1/2″ paper margins and on one side of bamboo frame. Place glued side of frame on back side of picture, and fold glued paper margins over thread. At top, bottom, and one-third of way up center bamboo stick, glue scrap strips of paper as reinforcement.

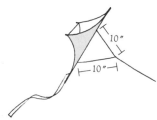

5. When glue is dry, make small hole in paper where bamboo pieces cross. Poke 22″ piece of kite string through hole from picture side and tie around bamboo pieces; tie other end to stick near bottom of picture. Tie one end of ball of kite string to midpoint of this loop. (In strong winds, retie knot 1″ or so above midpoint.)

6. For tail, glue one end of paper strip along bamboo extending at bottom. (A piece of rope may be used instead.) To better catch the wind, tie a string tautly between side bamboo ends so sides bow in on back side of picture. Adjust tail length for optimal flight.

Instructions for Warrior Kite begin on p. 133.

TOY TOPS

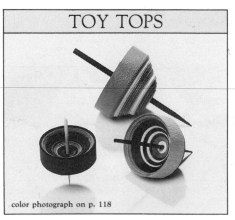

color photograph on p. 118

MATERIALS (makes 1)

colored paper: 1 strip, 1/2″ × 42″   **bamboo skewer (painted)**

NOTE: Striped tops can be made by using shorter strips of different colored papers; attach each strip to the next with glue. Vary the width and/or length of the paper strip(s) to make different sizes of tops.

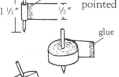

glue

1. Glue one end of paper strip to bamboo skewer near the pointed end. Roll paper strip tightly around stick.

glue

2. Glue down end of paper strip. Cut off skewer (not pointed end) to whatever length you like, leaving enough to grip.

3. Press down on inner coils of paper to mold top into desired shape.

BATTLEDORE AND SHUTTLECOCK

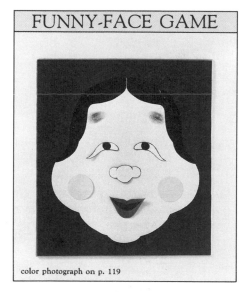

color photograph on p. 118

MATERIALS

wood: 1 board, ½″ × 5″ × 15″

soapberry seed (or any round, hard ¾″ dia. nut)

chicken or pigeon feathers: 3 (or 5)

fabric dye

bamboo skewer

NOTE: Use paulownia or any other lightweight, easily worked wood for the battledore.

1. Draw battledore (paddle) shape on board. First drill out at points marked with a dot, to enable clean cutting around sharp corners. Then saw out battledore with a jigsaw.

2. Sand edges smooth, and paint decoration on one side. The other, playing side is left undecorated.

3. Drill a hole in the seed. Color feathers with fabric dye. Apply glue to quill end of feathers and insert in hole, arranging so feathers arch out from center. Cut off short piece of bamboo skewer and glue it in hole to wedge in feathers.

FUNNY-FACE GAME

color photograph on p. 119

MATERIALS

heavy white paper: 8″ × 9″

red mat board: 9 ½″ × 10 ¾″

heavy cream-color paper: 8 ½″ × 9 ½″

red paper: 1 ½″ × 2 ½″

black paper: 5″ × 8″

pink paper: 1 ½″ × 3″

NOTE: Japanese gold-edged *shikishi* (fancy stiff paper for brushwork) may be substituted for the mat board, as was done for the game photographed.

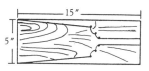

1. Draw face with pencil on heavy white paper. Cut out around face.

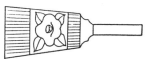

2. Place white face on cream-color paper and trace. Cut out face shape. Cut out eyes, cheeks, nose, etc., from white paper face for use as patterns. Trace nose on cream paper and cut out.

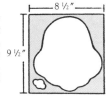

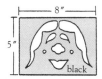

3. Trace patterns of hair, eyes, pupils, nose, and mouth on black paper, and cut out. Trim mouth to be slightly smaller than traced pattern.

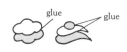

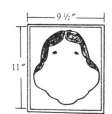

4. Trace mouth pattern on red paper and cut out (making mouth opening this time); glue over black mouth piece. Trace and cut eyes from white paper, making them slightly smaller than black eye pieces; glue together black, white, and pupil for each eye. Trace and cut out cheeks from pink paper. Glue cream-color nose piece over black.

5. Glue cream-color face shape to red posterboard. Glue on black hair. To draw eyebrows, rub black pencil or charcoal on fingertip and smudge on.

Setsubun

The last winter day according to the seasonal markers is *setsubun*, February 3 or 4. It is always obvious when *setsubun* is near, for on grocery store shelves devil masks begin to appear, paired, strangely enough, with bags of dried soybeans. Don't expect some American trick-or-treat, though: the beans are for throwing, to cast out the demons of illness and misfortune.

Families perform the traditional ceremony of *setsubun* on the last evening of winter. The soybeans are parched and placed in a small wooden box of a type traditionally used for measuring volume. The head of the household then scatters the beans inside and outside the home to the chant of *Oni wa soto! Fuku wa uchi*, or "Out with the demons! In with good luck!" Each family member eats the number of beans equal to his age.

Temples and shrines also cast out their demons on this day and, in an effort to attract people to the ceremony, often invite actors, baseball stars, and other celebrities born with the appropriate horoscope to do the bean tossing. Some of the visitors may ask to have an exorcism performed to avert misfortune. Or, they can buy a picture of the *takara-bune*, the ship that carries the seven gods of good fortune. Placed under one's pillow at night, the picture ensures that one can start out on the first day of spring with an auspicious dream.

The association of *setsubun* with bean tossing is now almost automatic, although the word itself refers merely to the division between the seasons, there being four such days throughout the year. As turning points, all are dangerous days, but only the day when winter turns to spring is now marked by a special protective ceremony. The reason for this is simple. Under the lunar calendar, this day was much closer to New Year's Day than it is now, and so the ceremonies associated with it were part of the important work of purification that each family had to perform to welcome the *toshigami* properly.

Other means are also used to keep demons out at *setsubun*. The front door can be embellished by a branch of holly with a grilled fish head stuck on one of the twigs so that the combination of sharp spines and stink will ward off evil spirits. Garlic is also an effective demon repellant.

Setsubun attained its present form somewhere between the fifteenth and seventeenth centuries. One of its roots was in the *tsuina* ceremony, originally a court ceremony but now performed by temples and shrines. In *tsuina*, demons that bring disease and disaster are symbolically cast out by shooting a reed arrow with a peach-wood bow. Another forerunner was *sanmai*, a ritual offering to baser spirits in which rice was scattered in the shrine grounds. Families took up the practice, too, using beans instead of rice, and eventually the exorcism of demons and the tossing of beans combined into today's *setsubun* ceremony.

The demons depicted in the masks sold at *setsubun* are called *oni*. Their faces are usually red and horned, like Satan's, but they look more wild and ferocious than evil. They are nevertheless powerful and violent, with complex natures that sometimes permit them to do good. While they can bring bountiful harvests and good fortune, and be worshiped as gods, they can also unpredictably cause destruction and pain. Perhaps this duality suggests our own duality. Perhaps those casting out demons on the eve of the new spring are symbolically cleansing themselves of their own evil sides, to start the year again in peace and love.

Setsubun's bean-tossing ceremony inspired these crafts: miniature bean dolls (instructions on p. 124), a demon mask (p. 124), and hexagonal boxes (p. 125) designed to resemble the sturdy measuring boxes that hold beans for the ceremony.

BEAN DOLLS

color photograph on p. 123

MATERIALS (makes 1)

dried soybeans: 4

patterned paper: ¾″ × 1 ¼″

gold paper: ⅛″ × 2 ½″

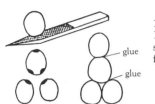

1. File 3 beans at one point and 1 bean at three points, as shown. Glue beans together at filed points.

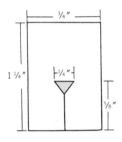

2. Cut front opening and neck triangle in patterned paper to make kimono.

3. Dress beans in kimono and trim paper so it barely shows the two base beans in front and touches the ground in back; the doll should stand on its own. Overlap front edges slightly and glue together.

4. Knot gold paper strip and trim ends to about ½″ each. Glue to front of kimono.

5. Paint in hair with sumi or India ink.

DEMON MASK

color photograph on p. 123

MATERIALS

plasticine (oil-based nondrying modeling clay): 4-6 lbs.

plaster of Paris: 3 lbs.

white paper (washi recommended): several sheets

heavy paper: 2 pieces, each 1 ½″ × 2″

newspaper   **gesso**   **poster paints**

1. Knead the clay on a smooth board until it reaches an easily workable consistency.

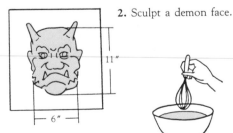

2. Sculpt a demon face.

3. Place plaster of Paris in a bowl and add water to barely cover. Stir gently with whisk about 10 times.

4. Wait about 10 minutes, until plaster of Paris has begun to harden and has reached consistency of heavy cream. Then spoon an even layer of plaster, ½″ or so thick, on the clay base.

5. Wait 30-40 minutes, until plaster is hard. Tap corners of board with a hammer to unstick mask. Remove all clay from inside of plaster mold with spoon and fingers.

6. Tear up white paper into strips, dip in water, and neatly apply one layer all over inside of mold. Dilute some glue to consistency slightly thicker than milk. Dip strips of newspaper into glue and apply about four layers to mold. Finish with layer of white paper strips dipped in glue.

7. Allow paper to dry thoroughly (about 24 hours), and then remove from mold.

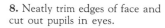

8. Neatly trim edges of face and cut out pupils in eyes.

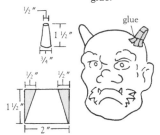

9. Make two conical cylinders (horns) from heavy paper, glue seam, and firmly attach to mask with glue-backed strips of white paper. Glue on paper strip to close opening at top of each horn.

10. Paint mask with gesso thinned with water. When dry, smooth surface of face with sandpaper. Paint on a demon's face. To wear, make holes near ears and tie piece of elastic or two strings or ribbons to each ear; tie string ends firmly behind head.

HEXAGONAL BOXES

color photograph on p. 123

MATERIALS

FOR SMALL BOX

cardboard:
1 piece, 1 7/8″ × 6 3/4″
2 strips, each 3/8″ × 7 1/2″
6 rectangles, each 1 1/2″ × 1 7/8″
circle, 3″ dia.

patterned paper:
1 strip, 2 1/8″ × 9 1/2″
1 circle, 3″ dia.

white paper:
1 strip, 2″ × 7 1/4″
1 circle, 3″ dia.
1 circle, 3 3/4″ dia.

FOR LARGE BOX

cardboard:
1 strip, 1 3/4″ × 9 3/4″
2 strips, each 3/8″ × 10 1/2″
6 rectangles, each 1 1/4″ × 2″
1 circle, 4″ dia.

patterned paper:
1 strip, 2″ × 12 1/4″
1 circle, 3 3/4″ dia.

white paper:
1 strip, 1 7/8″ × 9 7/8″
1 circle, 4″ dia.
1 circle, 4 1/2″ dia.

1. Measure off large piece of cardboard as shown. To facilitate folding, make shallow cuts along fold lines with an X-acto knife, being careful not to cut all the way through. Repeat for both cardboard strips.

SMALL BOX

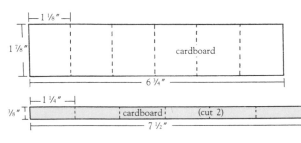

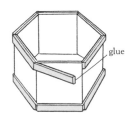

2. Fold large piece of cardboard into hexagon, with cut fold lines on outside, and glue cardboard strips to its exterior along top and bottom edges.

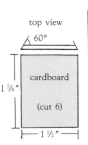

3. Bevel long edges of six cardboard rectangles at 60° angle, using the edge of a triangular rule as a guide. Glue to exterior walls of hexagon made in step 2.

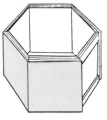

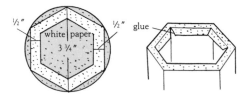

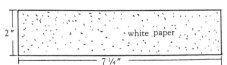

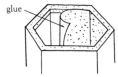

4. Cut larger circle of white paper into a hexagonal ring using a compass. Glue to top rim of hexagonal box. Snip into protruding white paper at inside corners of box, fold down to inside walls, and glue.

5. Glue strip of white paper to inside of box, aligning top edge of paper with lip of box. Snip (at corners) into paper extending out bottom of box, fold flat under bottom rim of box, and glue.

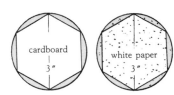

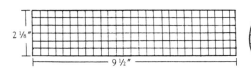

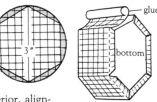

6. Cut cardboard circle and remaining white paper circle into hexagons. Glue white paper to cardboard and then glue the assembly to bottom of box made in step 5 with white paper on inside.

7. Glue rectangle of patterned paper to box exterior, aligning with top edge of box. Snip into excess at bottom corners, fold under, and glue down to bottom. Cut patterned paper circle into hexagon and glue to bottom exterior of box.

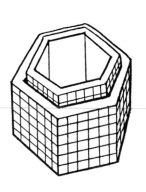

LARGE BOX

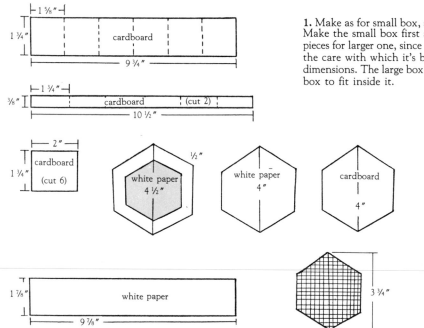

1. Make as for small box, substituting pieces sized as shown. Make the small box first and measure it before cutting out pieces for larger one, since the thickness of the cardboard and the care with which it's been measured will affect the final dimensions. The large box should be big enough for the small box to fit inside it.

STANDING DOLLS

color photograph on p. 19

MATERIALS

FOR EACH DOLL

head: same as for Genji Dolls (p. 20)

FOR LADY

collar:
pink paper, 1″ × 2 ½″

hair:
black paper, ¼″ × 5 ½″

kimono:
patterned paper, 4″ × 6 ¼″
1 strip pink paper, ¼″ × 3 ½″

FOR SAMURAI

collar: light-green paper, 1″ × 2 ½″   **cap:** gold paper, ¾″ × ¾″

kimono: 2 sheets patterned paper, 4 ¾″ × 9 ½″ and 5 ½″ × 5 ½″

LADY   **1.** Make head and attach collar, following procedures in steps 1–2 for Genji Dolls. (Collar is only one layer and slightly wider than Genji Doll's.)

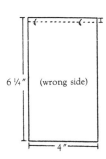

2. Fold down top edge of patterned paper.

3. Fold kimono around head in order of arrows, gluing head in place. Glue seam closed.

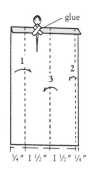

4. Wrap 3 ½″ pink strip around kimono, about one-third of the way from top, gluing to kimono and gluing overlapping ends together in back. Fold back bottom of kimono at angle.

5. Glue hair strip to back of head.

SAMURAI   **1.** Follow step 1 above, substituting collar paper for samurai.

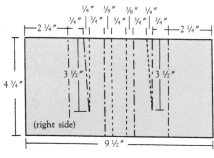

2. Pleat large patterned paper to make *hakama* (kimono overskirt). Glue overlapping edges together in back.

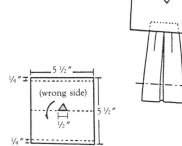

3. Cut triangular opening in other sheet of patterned paper and fold. Slip over doll's head, gluing in place.

4. Glue *hakama* between bottom edges of kimono top. Glue bottom edges of kimono top together. Fold back bottom of *hakama.*

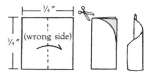

5. To make cap, fold gold paper in half, trim off corner, and glue edges together. Glue to samurai's head (rounded corner facing front) and shape by twisting top gently.

EGGSHELL FIGURINES *(cont. from p. 38)*

color photograph on p. 35

BENKEI

MATERIALS

body base: same as for Momotaro (p. 37)

underkimono: (A′) single-color paper, 1 ½″ × 6 ¼″

kimono: (A) 3 pieces patterned paper, 1 ½″ × 6 ¼″ and (for sleeves) two of 1 ½″ × 3″

hakama: (B) 2 pieces patterned paper, 1 ½″ × 6 ¼″ and 2″ dia. circle

vest:
(C) patterned paper, 3 ½″ × 5″
3 strips scrap patterned paper, ¼″ × 5 ½″ and two of ¼″ × 1 ⅛″
4 circles white paper, each ½″ dia.

accessories:
2 pieces black paper, ¼″ × 2 ⅛″ and 1″ × 1″ (for cap)
white string, 5″ long
thin white paper, 1 ⅛″ × 9″

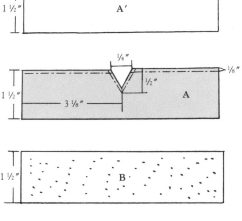

1. Follow steps 1–6 for Momotaro figurine to make eggshell body, substituting papers for Benkei. In step 5, first glue on strip of paper A′, then glue A over it, placing notches in center front.

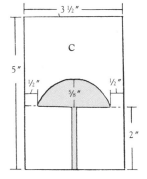

2. Cut and fold vest from paper C as shown. Dress figurine in it.

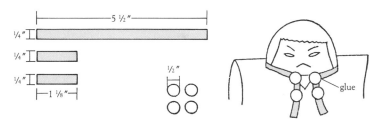

3. Glue on scrap patterned paper strips around neck opening. Paint in face and hair. Glue four white paper circles to collar as shown.

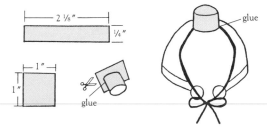

4. Roll black strip for cap into a cylinder, glue closed, then glue to center of black square. Cut off protruding edges of black square to make top of cylindrical cap. Tie white string around doll's head, positioning bow under chin. Secure in place with dab of glue on top of head and under chin. Glue on hat.

5. Write tiny calligraphy on the thin paper to make a handscroll. Roll up one end of scroll an inch or so. Glue rolled end to tip of doll's left sleeve. Glue other end, with writing facing doll, to right sleeve tip.

SHIBARAKU

MATERIALS

body base: same as for Momotaro (p. 37)

underkimono: (A′) 3 pieces paper, 1 ½″ × 6 ¼″ and two of ½″ × 1 ¼″

kimono: (A) 3 pieces patterned paper, 1 ½″ × 6 ¼″ and (for sleeves) two of 2″ × 5″

outer kimono:
(B) 6 pieces patterned paper, 1 ½″ × 6 ¼″, 2″ dia. circle, and (for sleeves) four of 2 ½″ × 2 ½″
2 pieces white paper, each 1 ¾″ × 1 ¾″

accessories:
4 pieces white paper (for belt), ½″ × ¼″, ½″ × ¾″, and two of ¼″ × 6 ¼″
white paper, ½″ × ½″ (for sword)
patterned paper, ¼″ × 1 ⅝″ (for sword handle)
gold paper, 2 ⅛″ × 3 ½″ (for sword and fan)
gold metallic paper, 1″ × 2 ⅜″ (for cap)
purple cord, 5″ long
white seine twine, 14″ long

1. Follow steps 1–5 for Momotaro figurine to make eggshell body, substituting papers for Shibaraku. In step 5, first glue on strip of paper A′, then glue A over it, placing notches in center front.

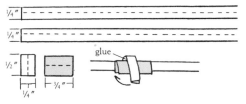

2. Fold the white paper pieces for belt as shown. First glue one of the long pieces around top edge of paper B on figurine, overlapping and gluing ends. Repeat with other long piece, placing it slightly below first belt. Make a "bow" out of smaller pieces, and glue it to middle of lower belt.

3. To make sleeves, fold edges of remaining pieces of paper A, curving two corners. To each sleeve glue a rectangle of paper A′, folded in half, so that its edge will show slightly at the wrist when sleeves are folded. Attach sleeves as in step 6 for Momotaro figurine.

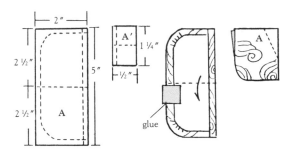

4. To make outer kimono sleeves, fold in edges of four squares of paper B and glue together in pairs, folded edges facing in. Cut white paper for outer kimono as shown, glue in concentric squares to these sleeves, and attach sleeves to body under inner-kimono sleeves with a dab of glue. These lower sleeves represent an outer kimono thrown off the shoulders but still cinched at the waist.

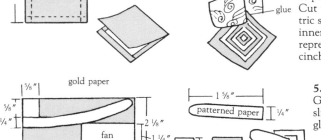

5. Cut out sword (and fan) pieces. Glue handle on top of hilt. Glue white hollow square to square of gold paper and cut a slit in the center. Insert sword handle in slit and secure with glue. Glue sword to body beneath left sleeve.

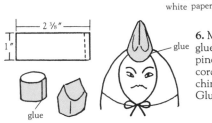

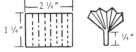

6. Make a cylinder from gold paper for cap, glue overlapping ends together, and then pinch in top edges as shown. Tie purple cord around head, positioning bow under chin. Glue under bow and on top of head. Glue hat in place.

7. Accordion-fold gold paper piece for fan, gluing together folds along bottom ¼″. Glue to top corner of right sleeve.

8. Tie white string in big bow and glue to back of figurine at top edge of kimono.

color photograph on p. 47

BRIDE DOLL

MATERIALS

head: same as for Shimada Doll (p. 48)

hair ornaments:
silver paper, ½″ × 1 ½″
2 pieces single-strand gold *mizuhiki*, each 2″ long
stiff yellow paper, 1″ × 1 ¾″
thin white paper, 1″ × 5″

mid-layers and underkimono:
4 sheets white paper, each 4 ½″ × 9″
light pink paper, 4 ¼″ × 8 ½″
white paper, 1″ × 3 ¾″ (for underkimono collar)

kimono:
white textured paper, 4 ½″ × 11″
white paper, 4 ½″ × 9″ (for lining)
light pink paper, 1″ × 4 ½″ (for collar)

obi (sash):
3 pieces white textured paper, 3 ½″ × 3″ (for front),
   2 ½″ × 7 ½″ (for bow), and 1 ½″ × 3 ¼″ (for knot)
white paper, ⅛″ × 3 ½″ (for obi cord)

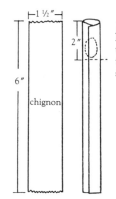

1. Follow steps 1–9 for Shimada Doll. Wrinkle the chignon piece until 1 ½″ wide, place bit of cotton batting as shown, and fold over sides of paper.

2. Fold down top and tie string around cotton padding to make chignon.

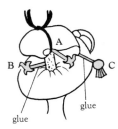

3. Wrap silver paper around base of chignon and glue in place.

4. Insert long end of chignon piece through hole in coil, positioning chignon loop at back of head. Bend short end of chignon and insert tip into hole; glue in place. Holding the two *mizuhiki* strands together, tie them in square knot around chignon, covering string.

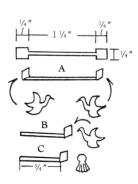

5. Cut out hair ornaments from stiff yellow paper as shown. Bend up ends and glue on birds and cutout representing tassel.

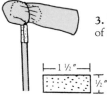

6. Glue resulting three ornaments in place as follows: Piece A goes horizontally through side opening of chignon. B goes in back, near silver paper at base of chignon. C is glued to coil to right of front hair.

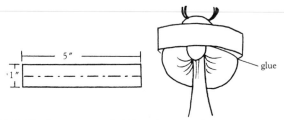

7. Fold white paper in half lengthwise and shape into a ring that rests on coil, glue ends together in rear.

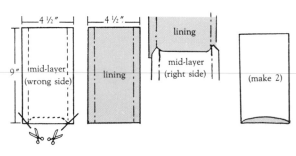

8. Make kimono by attaching lining to textured kimono paper as in steps 21–23 for Shimada Doll. Then make two mid-layers (kimonos), using two 4 ½″ × 9″ sheets for each and joining the sheets as in steps 21–22.

9. Fold pink collar in half lengthwise and glue to inside top edge of kimono so that collar's folded edge extends slightly above top of kimono.

glue

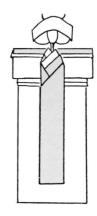

10. Glue the two mid-layers to inside of kimono so that mid-layer bottom edges extend slightly below kimono bottom.

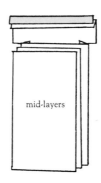

mid-layers

11. Make pink underkimono with white collar, and wrap around doll, following steps 19-20 for Shimada Doll. Dress doll in kimono, following steps 24-25.

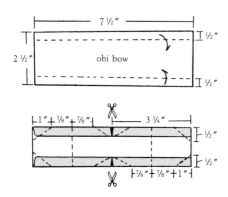

obi bow

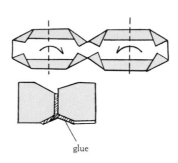

glue

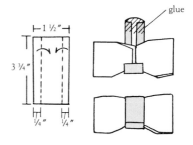

glue

12. Fold in edges of paper for obi bow. Snip in ½″ at midpoint of top and bottom edges, and make diagonal folds as shown.

13. Fold both ends to middle. Glue down.

14. Fold in long edges of paper for obi knot. Glue around obi bow as shown.

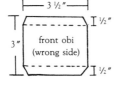

front obi
(wrong side)

15. Snip off corners of paper for obi front, and fold in long edges.

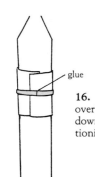

glue

16. Wrap obi front around doll, overlapping ends in back, and glue down. Glue obi cord around obi, positioning joint in back.

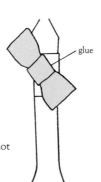

glue

17. Glue on obi bow and knot at angle, as shown.

color photograph on p. 66

FAN WITH LEAF

MATERIALS

balsa wood:
(A) 1 stick, $\frac{1}{16}'' \times \frac{1}{2}'' \times 6\frac{1}{2}''$
(B) 1 stick, $\frac{1}{16}'' \times \frac{1}{2}'' \times 3''$
(C) 3 sticks, $\frac{1}{16}'' \times \frac{1}{4}'' \times 10''$
(D) 2 sticks, $\frac{1}{16}'' \times \frac{1}{4}'' \times 5''$
(E) 2 sticks, $\frac{1}{16}'' \times \frac{1}{4}'' \times 8''$

white paper:
2 sheets, each $10'' \times 10''$
1 strip, $2'' \times 24''$

thin paper: $10'' \times 10''$

fern (or other thin leaf)

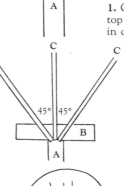

1. Cut a tab with an X-acto knife in top of stick A. Cut a matching groove in center of stick B. Glue together.

2. Glue C sticks on top of tab joint as shown.

3. Glue D and E sticks in between as shown, tapering their ends with an X-acto knife so they fit neatly between sticks glued in step 2. Cut off ends of crossbar B that protrude beyond outermost sticks.

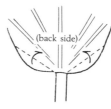

4. Lightly dampen two sheets of white paper with atomizer. Glue paper to fan following steps 7–8 of Fan with Color Gradation. Be sure to cover the spokes entirely.

5. Place leaf between two sheets of scrap paper and press flat with an iron.

6. While fan is still damp, spread glue evenly on paper of one side of fan. Apply glue to both sides of pressed leaf and place on fan. Dampen thin paper and place on leaf side of fan, smoothing it in place.

(back side)

7. When fan is completely dry, trim edges of paper and ribs to make circular shape. Fold up bottom edges of paper to side opposite leaf, and glue down.

THIMBLES (cont. from p. 85)

color photograph on p. 82

SMALL THIMBLE

MATERIALS

fabric: $1\frac{1}{4}'' \times 3''$

cotton batting: a small piece

cardboard: $\frac{3}{8}'' \times 2\frac{1}{4}''$

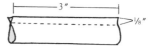

1. Fold fabric lengthwise, right side on inside, and stitch together along long edge, leaving a $\frac{1}{8}''$ seam allowance.

2. Turn right-side out. Insert cardboard, centering in tube, and stuff cotton batting between cardboard and top fabric.

3. Gather together fabric at both ends and sew closed. Curve into ring, concealing long seam on inside of thimble, and sew ends together.

color photograph on p. 118

WARRIOR KITE

MATERIALS

split bamboo:
3 pieces, each 1/16″ dia. × 35″

white paper:
1 sheet, 20″ × 15″
2 strips, each 1 1/2″ × 30″–50″

strong cotton thread

kite string

NOTE: Asterisks indicate the type of knot required. (See diagram to left for instructions.) Generally, * knots are for thread, ** knots are for kite string.

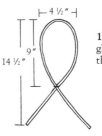

1. Bend one piece of bamboo as shown, glue joint, then tie securely with thread.

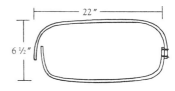

2. Glue remaining bamboo together as shown, and tie ends securely with thread.

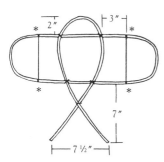

3. Combine the two constructed pieces as shown. Glue and then tie at points of intersection. Tie threads tautly across frame at points indicated.

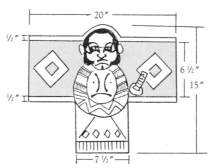

4. Paint a warrior or other figure on sheet of paper and cut out, leaving a 1/2″ margin on top and bottom edges of sleeves.

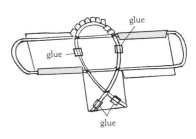

5. Spread glue on one side of bamboo frame (except for sleeve ends), on string spans, and on undecorated side of 1/2″ paper margins. Place frame on paper. Clip into margin around head of figure. Fold over all glued paper margins. Glue scrap strips of paper as reinforcement at points indicated.

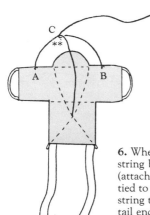

6. When glue is dry, tie 24″ piece of kite string between points A and B of frame (attach about where support threads are tied to frame). Tie one end of ball of kite string to point C, leaving a 12″ tail. Tie tail end to point D (make hole in paper, pass string through from picture side, tie to frame joint). (In strong winds, retie so tail C-D is longer than A-C and B-C.) For tails, glue two strips of paper to bottom corners of kite.

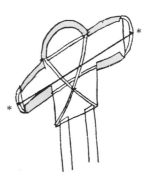

7. On reverse side, stretch a string across kite, tying to bamboo frame at points indicated, to curve kite slightly.

Appendix: List of Suppliers

WHERE TO BUY JAPANESE PAPER

Japanese paper, or *washi*, is available at large art-supply stores and Oriental import stores. The following shops are a partial listing.

AIKO'S ART MATERIALS IMPORT
714 North Wabash Avenue
Chicago, IL 60611
(312)943-0745

AMSTERDAM ART
1013 University Avenue
Berkeley, CA 94710
(415)548-9663

CANDO K. HOSHINO
1541 Clement Street
San Francisco, CA 94118
(415)752-1636

KABUKI GIFTS AND IMPORTS
11355 Santa Monica Blvd.
W. Los Angeles, CA 90025
(213)477-2663

KAREL ART MATERIALS
737 Canal Street
Stamford, CT 06902
(203)348-8996

KASURI DYEWORKS
1959 Shattuck Avenue
Berkeley, CA 94704
(415)841-4509

KATE'S ART SUPPLY
2 W. 13th Street
New York, NY 10011
(212)675-6406

KINOKUNIYA
1581 Webster Street
San Francisco, CA 94115
(415)567-7625

LEE'S ART SHOP
220 W. 57th Street
New York, NY 10019
(212)247-0110

NEW YORK CENTRAL ART SUPPLY
62 3rd Avenue
New York, NY 10003
(212)473-7705

SAM FLAX
55 E. 55th Street New York, NY 10022
(212)620-3060
15 Park Row, New York, NY 10038
(212)620-3030
25 E. 28th Street, New York, NY 10016
(212)620-3040
747 3rd Avenue, New York, NY 10017
(212)620-3050
12 W. 20th Street, New York, NY 10011
(212)620-3038

WHERE TO BUY MIZUHIKI

Mizuhiki are available at Oriental import stores like the ones below.

AIKO'S ART MATERIALS IMPORT
714 North Wabash Avenue
Chicago, IL 60611
(312)943-0745

KABUKI GIFTS AND IMPORTS
11355 Santa Monica Blvd.
W. Los Angeles, CA 90025
(213)477-2663

ZEN ORIENTAL BOOKSTORE
521 5th Avenue, New York, NY 10175
(212)697-0840
115 W. 57th Street, New York, NY 10019
(212)582-4622

Index

Acknowledgments

CRAFT PROJECT INSTRUCTIONS: Shiro Mimoto, Kazutoshi Omoda, and Michiko Ito prepared the original instructions in Japanese. Michiko Uchiyama, Pamela Pasti, and Ruth S. McCreery translated and adapted them.

PHOTO CREDITS: The companies and photographers who supplied photographs for this book are: Dandi Photo, pp. 11, 39, 71, 91; Tsuneo Hayashida, p. 94 (crane); Keizo Kaneko, p. 95 (*sukiyaki*), p. 109 (bamboo decorations and a lacquer set for serving saké); Kugetsu Inc., p. 32 (Boys' Day dolls); Masayoshi Kurahashi, p. 75 (rice plant); Tooru Kurobe, p. 45 (*yosenabe*); Yuji Matsubayashi, p. 42 (dragonfly), p. 74 (Japanese maple); Katsuhiko Mizuno, p.46 (bamboo); Shinji Takano, p. 14 (bush warbler); and Kumeo Yamada, p. 43 (grilled sweetfish). The remaining illustrations are from the Kodansha Ltd. photo library.

The publisher would like to thank the following for supplying objects to be photographed: Ogimura Shikki-ten for the lacquer lunch boxes, tray, and saké cups on pp. 26, 27; Masuda-ya for the lacquer stands on pp. 18, 19; Mitsubo for the pig-shaped mosquito-coil burner on p. 67; Keiko Hayashi for the glass dish on p. 67; Kamehan for the gourd decanter on p. 27; and Miwa Takano for the flowers on the front jacket.

The publisher also wishes to express gratitude to Yorozu-en for providing information on growing ferns, to Taiko Tsutsui for preparing the chestnut rice on p. 75, to Masaru Doi for preparing the New Year's dishes on p. 107, and to Kasuri Dyeworks for information on doorway curtains.